To Make the World Intelligible

A Scientist's Journey

FRANKLIN M. HAROLD, PhD

 FriesenPress

Suite 300 - 990 Fort St
Victoria, BC, V8V 3K2
Canada

www.friesenpress.com

ISBN
978-1-5255-0018-3 (Hardcover)
978-1-5255-0019-0 (Paperback)
978-1-5255-0020-6 (eBook)

1. BIOGRAPHY & AUTOBIOGRAPHY, SCIENCE & TECHNOLOGY

Distributed to the trade by The Ingram Book Company

Table of Contents

Dedication..v

Acknowledgements vii

Preface..ix

Part I: As I Remember it

1: What's Bred in the Bone 1

2: Coming into the Country 9

3: Becoming a Scientist...............................17

4: Worlds to Conquer..................................27

5: Eccentric, with a Touch of Genius 49

6: When the Going was Good 59

7: Sailing to Byzantium 83

Part II: The Perplexing Phenomenon of Life

Introduction 105

8: Strange Objects....................................109

9: Cells, Genes, and Molecules.......................119

10: The Tapestry That Weaves Itself...................133

Epilogue: Desiderata..................................155

Notes...159

Glossary..167

Dedication

To the women in my life: My mother, Hermine Harold, who was born in the age of horse and buggy, lived to fly in a jet airliner, and put my feet on the right track; my wife, Ruth, who shared the highs and lows recollected here; our daughter, Lynn Stephanie, teacher and wilderness traveler in Alaska; and our granddaughter, Jordan, who is now unfurling her own wings.

Acknowledgements

Some of the headings look familiar because they were stolen from the works of others. Phillip Ball, Robertson Davies, Max Ehrmann, John McPhee, Evelyn Waugh, and William Butler Yeats, thank you.

I write by hand and relied on Jennifer Chubb to turn yellow pages of scribbling into neat typescript. Thank you, I could not have done this without your help. Special thanks are due to Teala Beischer of FriesenPress, who patiently guided me through the publishing process.

Friends, neighbors, and colleagues engaged with this project and shared their reactions. Robert Adriance, Ginny and Steve Burger, Elaine ("Sunnie") Gordon, Ruth Harold, Patty and Jim Larson, Mary Ann Kirkpatrick, Roger Olstad, Diana and Sam Spencer, and Fred Tuttle, thank you all. The recollections and reflections expressed here are my own, warts and all.

Preface

During the latter half of the 20th century, the staid science of biology was radically transformed from a largely descriptive pursuit focused on living organisms into an intensely experimental one centered upon their molecular constituents. As biology became ever more integrated with physics and chemistry, fundamental questions that could barely be formulated before the Second World War quickly found answers. Four decades sufficed to work out the structures of biological molecules, the pathways by which they are synthesized, the architecture of cells, the mechanism of heredity, and how energy is captured and utilized. The expectation that our deepening understanding of how living things function would translate into practical applications to medicine, agriculture, and industry attracted generous funding and opened up a wide range of professional opportunities. Science, as the search for truth about the nature and workings of our world, basked in public confidence and support. This was a unique era, never to be repeated. It was my great good fortune to come of age early in that upheaval, to engage with basic biological science during its heyday both as an observer of the process and as an active participant, and to make my own small contribution to the great metamorphosis.

At the personal level also, this is an account of a fortunate life, one touched by great events but not overwhelmed by them. Thanks to my parents' foresight, we escaped both the holocaust and Israel's endless war with the Arabs. Diabetes, the family scourge for four generations, skipped me. Too young for World War II, too old for Vietnam, the United States gave me freedom and opportunity to set my own course. I found my vocation early and never looked back. My wife Ruth and I have recently celebrated our 62nd wedding anniversary, capping a loving and stable marriage that matured into an enduring friendship. The working years were followed by sixteen more of zestful retirement, combining family, travel, and creative activities. For sixty years, we took advantage of every opportunity to hike and to travel and managed to see most of what the world offers to lovers of antiquity and the high mountains. But the golden years do not last forever. I have turned 87 now, am significantly hampered by the aftermath of a stroke, and can see how the game ends. With the active years clearly drawing to a close, it is timely to pull together the threads of this life and to put the pattern in the context of time, place, and circumstances.

An autobiography is an exercise in self-indulgence. Does anyone care about my particular experiences and reflections? I am respectable but neither important nor famous; many others have contributed more than I, and thought far more deeply. To borrow a memorable quip from Winston Churchill (referring to a rival politician), I consider myself "a modest man with much to be modest about". But I am also one bit of flotsam in the great tide driven by the rise of fascism in Europe that shaped the world we live in today, and I make a good example of science as a profession and a way of life. By putting flesh on the bare bones of a standard *curriculum vitae,* one gains some insight into the dialogue between the sweep of history's currents and the personal choices we are free to make. I made my own way into science and found that it gave meaning and purpose to my whole life, as thousands of others have found before me. If there is more to these musings than the personal need to scratch the writer's itch, it is because they capture an echo of the glory years of basic cellular and molecular biology, when small science tackled the grand questions and gained deep insight into the workings and nature of life.

This book is divided into two distinct parts. The first is about me – who I am and how I got to be that way. The second turns to more general matters. I hold that the true use of science is not to solve mankind's mounting problems but to make the world intelligible. As a biologist, I have for some years been obsessed with the peculiar and baffling phenomenon of life. The nature of life and its relationship to the inanimate world seems to me the central problem of biology, and my objective in the second half of this book is to consider how far we have come towards a rational understanding of life as a phenomenon of nature.

PART I: AS I REMEMBER IT

1: What's Bred in the Bone

I don't want to live in the past, but I want to live in a present that is rooted in the past. Only as an extension of the past does the present cease to be a chaos of unmeaning.
　—Philip Glazebrook, *Journey to Khiva*

I was born in March 1929 in Frankfurt-am-Main, Germany, the only child of a bourgeois Jewish family, and named Wolfgang Leo Max Isaac – Wolfgang for Goethe, Leo for my deceased grandfather, and Max for my mother's brother who served in the German army in World War I and died of cholera in Romania. My father held a doctorate in economics, but his real interest was in anthropology. In those days, Jews were largely barred from the academic positions that he would have loved, but he made a good living as a co-owner of a successful small advertising agency. Mother, some years older, was born in Strasburg (German since the war of 1870); trained as a nurse, she tended wounded soldiers in the latter years of the First World War. That combination of alert intelligence and down-to-earth shrewdness would save all our lives.

They wore their Judaism lightly. Like most assimilated German Jews, my parents were fully integrated into the culture of their day, immersed in the history, literature, and music of Central Europe; "German citizens of Jewish faith", as the mantra had it. Religious observance played little part in their lives, but they were conscious of their ethnicity and cultural identity as Jews. In this respect, as in the pattern of life in general, I have largely upheld the family tradition. Papa earned his living as a businessman, but he was a scholar at heart and well read all across the humanities. I like to believe that I take after him, and that I have led my life as he would have chosen to lead his own. Ima (Hebrew for mother) was intelligent but not intellectual. I owe her a sturdy physique that lasted into my eighties, and perhaps some modicum of good judgment. Between them, they provided a secure and supportive childhood upon which I could build, and we in turn tried to do the same for our daughter.

They also kept informed, watched the rise of Nazism with mounting alarm, and took timely action. Hitler was elected Chancellor of Germany in the spring of 1933, and that fall, we moved to Strasbourg – French since 1918. But we could not settle there permanently because the French government was leery of German nationals living in the long-disputed Alsace. We could have moved into the interior of France; had we done that we would have been trapped. Instead, a year and a half later we left Europe for Palestine, at that time a League of Nations mandate within the British Empire. We were emigrants, not refugees, and free to take out money and personal belongings, packed into a huge crate or "lift". My parents were Zionists, but more significantly, they were imbued with the idea that in a world growing ever darker, the way to salvation lay in a return to the land. Neither had ever held a hoe, but after a short period of training, they joined the pioneer farming settlement of Nahariya, on the coast of northern Palestine. The area was almost wholly Arab, with its center in the medieval town of Acco (Acre) a few miles to the south.

Nahariya was not a kibbutz; we owned a plot of farmland and a simple house, but agricultural purchases and marketing were done communally. The settlers were all German Jews, many of them well educated but without experience with farming, and they found themselves unable to thrive in the soil and climate of coastal Palestine. After a few years, with bankruptcy staring many families in the face, the settlers of Nahariya decided collectively to abandon farming and turn the village into a holiday resort. The decision made good sense: With war-clouds gathering, people were no longer comfortable going to Europe, and the Middle East offered few alternatives. My father was put in charge of the transformation. He launched an advertising campaign and saw to it that visitors would find rooms to rent, a few restaurants, a lifeguard and shade on the beach, music on weekend evenings, and even a local library and museum. With its lovely sand beach and a view of the mountains of Galilee to the east, the venture prospered. Nahariya grew rapidly (more than 50,000 people live there today) and remains one of Israel's most popular seaside resorts.

Nahariya was an idyllic place in which to grow up. My arrival in 1935 made five children, so they opened a one-room school. Jews have traditionally valued education, and as the village grew, so did the school. We all spoke German, but the language of instruction was Hebrew, and we started on English by age 10. A small village offered plenty of "community" (sometimes rather too much), but with its progressive middle-class European culture it also provided books to read, a broad outlook on the world, classical music, and encouragement to learn. I became a voracious and omnivorous reader; within a couple of years I was fluent in English, thanks largely to Agatha Christie and Hercule Poirot. Let me emphasize that the Jews who settled in Palestine were not at all religious and rejected much of the traditional Jewish culture of the *shtetls*, the small towns of Eastern Europe. Their goal was to build a functioning modern society and someday an independent state. No one ever wore a prayer cap outside of services, and Marx loomed larger in their thinking than Moses.

Little Wolfgang, who had turned Leon in France, now morphed smoothly into Arieh. I picked up Hebrew in a matter of weeks during our training period. My parents slaved on their farm ("Two acres and independence", as the inspirational slogan had it), but I was free to run around barefoot, ride our donkey, go swimming (I excelled at that), and to absorb the spectacle of the Levant from the viewpoint of the Jews returning, after 2000 years of exile, to their biblical homeland. I quickly became fascinated with the ancient, intricate, colorful, and ambiguous social fabric of the Middle East. Our corner was quite typical – Arabs, Turks, British rulers, Jewish immigrants, Armenians, Druze, and Bosniaks all simmering in the same pot while fiercely retaining their individual identities. All around were the vestiges of those who had inhabited these lands before us: Crusader castles, Byzantine churches and an aqueduct, Roman and Phoenician cemeteries, thirty-five hundred years' worth of potsherds, and the flaked stone tools of ice-age hunters. I have never outgrown the fascination with that world and have returned to the Middle East many times, both in body and by armchair.

Events in the great world outside cast a shadow over our bucolic existence, but in retrospect it seems not to have been too dark. My immediate family all made it out of Germany, including my grandparents who lived with us in Nahariya. Of the holocaust then under way in Europe we knew little. For the most part, the war was noises off-stage, but we were in the path of German bombers striking at the oil refinery in Haifa, and once or twice they dropped a load on us. A far more serious threat arose when the Germans invaded North Africa in 1940, and Rommel's tanks drove towards the Nile. Had they succeeded, the entire Arab world would have risen against the British and the Jews, and we would have been slaughtered. I remember pensive walks at sunset to the tank-trap, a ditch dug at the edge of Nahariya and set with concrete teeth to stop the Panzers (my skeptical habit of mind may owe something to that ditch). I was too young to appreciate the gravity of the danger; only later did I realize how much we owed to the Poles and Aussies who held Tobruk and slowed Rommel's advance, to the Tommies who turned the tide at El Alamein, and to Winston Churchill who kept up Britain's spirit during a long, dark night.

Relations with our Arab neighbors were quite peaceful most of the time. They surely resented our encroachment on the land but also appreciated its benefits. For example, one of our neighbors in town was an ophthalmologist who built up an Arab practice; all day long his clinic was busy with mothers bringing their children to be treated for trachoma (a major cause of blindness). But in 1936, tensions broke into the open when the Arabs mounted an insurrection. (We called it "The

Riots", to Arabs it is their "First War of Independence".) Jewish settlements, including ours, came under attack; buses were ambushed, and people were killed. It took convoys of armored cars to re-open the road to Haifa. The riots were put down and quiet returned; but no one forgot that what happened once can come again. Few then realized that the Zionist project implied an inevitable and bitter conflict with the Arabs over the rightful ownership of that land.

The twig bent early towards science. As a child I collected seashells, fossils, and especially the bric-a-brac of the ancient past: stone-age hand axes, Phoenician pottery, and Roman coins (purchased by the kilo from an Arab jeweler in Acco and laboriously cleaned and identified). My first contribution to science, age 15, was a handwritten report to the Department of Antiquities in Jerusalem on what turned up when road construction cut across a corner of a small mound right on our beach. It prompted an archaeologist to come and have a look, and I got to work on the excavation of a Canaanite temple from the time of Abraham. I also helped rob a tomb (collector's lust, not science) and seriously considered becoming an archaeologist.

And then, aged about 16, I discovered chemistry. The initial impetus came from a popular book on "chemurgy", such matters as how fertilizer is made and what goes on in an oil refinery. By then I was attending Hugim High School in Haifa, which offered a secular Jewish curriculum to European standards but did not neglect science. High school education was private then, not public, and most students went to work once they had completed eight grades of elementary school. Within a few months, I was hooked on chemistry, and in need of a laboratory of my own. The solution was a disused outhouse at the rear of our property, left over from farming days. I put a board over the seat, fixed a barrel on the roof for water, cut down light bulbs for reaction vessels, and purchased chemicals from the local pharmacy (no chemistry kits then, but no prepackaged drugs either). A friendly engineer got his glassblower to make me a simple Liebig condenser, and I was on my way. A homemade microscope and an even cruder telescope completed the equipment, and by some miracle nothing ever blew up. Mr. Ephraim Joel, science teacher in Nahariya's elementary school, gave me the run of his extensive library of science books in both German and English. I sponged up chemistry, biology, and some physics, much of it way over my head but all fuel for a growing passion.

With the war winding down and the British Empire coming unglued, the Jews of Palestine began to plan for a future as an independent Jewish state. Strangely, the nationalistic fervor that engulfed almost all my schoolmates left me quite unmoved, and I do not fully understand why. One reason is that I could never swallow the claim that Jews hold exclusive rights to Palestine, superseding the claims of Arabs who have lived there for the past two thousand years; it made no sense to me then, and it makes no sense now. The other reason is that I was simply not turned on by the goal of creating a national home for the Jewish people. By then I had come to focus on a personal objective, to study science and do chemistry. My parents also had become disillusioned; they understood that the conflict with the Arabs would never end and were unwilling to risk their only son for a cause they could no longer believe in. Besides, my father's work in Nahariya was done, and he felt increasingly ill at ease with the strident nationalism of the emerging Israel. We were able to wrangle a visa on the German quota, and in November 1947, we sailed for the United States. The United Nations ordered the partition of Palestine while we were aboard ship, and the countdown began to independence and war.

When we left Palestine I was 18 years old, and in retrospect, I can see that my personality, attitudes, and interests were already shaped for life. I am a Jew – secular, detribalized, and nonobservant, but nevertheless Jewish by ethnicity and outlook. My attitude towards the state of Israel remains ambivalent. I reject the moral claim to the land, but then most peoples acquired their homeland by forcibly displacing earlier inhabitants, and I greatly admire the many achievements of the Jewish state. I am convinced that Israel will survive in the Arab Middle East only so long as it can deploy superior armed might, has the economy to support an outsize military, and has the ferocity to use it. I am also aware that all Jews, including those who reject Israel's moral pretensions, have benefited enormously from the respect that the small but combative state has generated. Science is still the pivot on which my life turns, but this nerdy preoccupation is softened by a love of nature and the outdoors and by a deep fondness for history and foreign places. I came away from the Middle East with a lifelong case of Anglophilia, a firm belief in the importance of government as an instrument of order and progress, and a profound sense of the uncertainty of life and the transience of all achievement. I still believe in charity and communal efforts to improve people's lives, but also in individual responsibility; and I am increasingly skeptical about the prospects for human betterment. After nearly 70 years as an American, I remain distinctly foreign: What's bred in the bone (to borrow a phrase from Robertson Davies) is the old world, not the new.

2: Coming into the Country

Traveler, there are no roads. Roads are made by walking.
—Joaquim Machado

New York, 1947 – 1952

Scientists are not born, they are made. Even those born into a supportive environment and blessed with the inclination towards science and a touch of talent must acquire the technical and social skills to function as scientists in the world of today. Academic credentials are indispensable for anyone who would gain admission to what has become a kind of priesthood. Each of us finds his or her own path into that company, and mine was no more haphazard than most others.

New York City was cold, grey, and bleak when we landed there in December 1947. Relatives had found an apartment for us in Washington Heights (uptown Manhattan), a neighborhood favored by German-speaking immigrants, and that became the setting for our own version of the incomers' experience. We took out "First Papers", the first step towards eventual citizenship. Arieh turned into Franklin (after President Roosevelt, who was immensely admired). We also changed the family name to conform to the choice made by my uncle, who had come to the United States some years earlier (his first name was Harald). I regret that now, but at the time it seemed desirable to go by a name that was not so blatantly Jewish. Mother quickly obtained work as a nurses' aide, but Papa had a very trying time finding his place; it was years before he began to earn a decent income. My goal was to study chemistry, but first there was a living to make.

I started as a bottle washer at Bios Laboratories, a small industrial firm that made organic chemicals and biochemicals for the growing research market. After a few months, I was promoted to the most junior of the chemists, responsible for simple preparations of my own. Being fluent in German, one of my chief duties was to look up things in *Beilstein*, a vast compendium of chemical information that filled an entire room at the Chemists Club in mid-Manhattan. It would be hard to overestimate the value of all this practical experience in being a chemist. After three years, in the wake of a laboratory fire that nearly sent us all to Kingdom Come, I found another job as a technician in the gastroenterology research laboratory at Mount Sinai Hospital. Dr. Max Adler was studying the chemistry of gastric mucus, an unappetizing slime of considerable physiological and medical importance. Dr. Adler soon became my mentor more than my boss. I also met Alexander Hollaender, head of the laboratory and noted as the author of a hypothesis to explain how the stomach secretes acid. They opened my first window into the world of scientific research, which I immediately found congenial.

It was CCNY, the City College of the College of the City of New York, which made it possible to pursue an academic course in chemistry while working nearly full time. CCNY was founded more than a century earlier to supply the economy of a growing industrial and mercantile city with educated workers of all kinds, and it continues to serve this mission to this day. An extraordinary number of prominent professionals, many of them scientists, owe their start to the "Harvard of the Poor". Tuition was free, but academic standards were high, thus attracting talented and ambitious students from all across New York's multi-cultural society and guaranteeing that they would find employment upon graduation. My contribution to the family budget could not be spared, so I enrolled in the evening session. I started out in chemical engineering, but quickly realized that I had neither aptitude nor inclination for that work. Fortunately, by then I had discovered that one could make a living as a chemist, and so I graduated in 1952 with a B.S. in chemistry (minor in geology) and confidence that I could marry and support a family. But that was not at all my inclination: I was eager to continue my studies and pursue a career in biochemistry.

My schedule left little time for collegiate fun and games, but two extracurricular activities still stand out. The City College Hiking Club introduced me to the hills, which remain an unsurpassed source of pleasure. The American Museum of Natural History became my comfort zone in the vast and impersonal city, sustaining my interest in archaeology and geology and turning my mind towards evolution. And when I was ready to move on, my favorite teacher at CCNY, Prof. Robert Goldberg, eased me into his pipeline to graduate school at the University of California at Berkeley. That summer, I went West for good.

On the Loose, 1952

The summer of 1952 is etched in my memory as a high point of my life. My hiking buddy Ralph Hathaway, who had also just finished college, was likewise at loose ends. He was bound for the Army, I for graduate school, but in the meantime, there was a whole summer without structure, obligations, and goals. Adventure beckoned, and we set out to explore the West with packs on our backs, very little money, and all the exuberant energy of youth. Nowadays such places as the Colorado Rockies and the Grand Canyon are standard destinations for a family vacation, and crawling with tourists. That was much less true 65 year ago, when the West was a very long way from the population centers of the East Coast and still held pockets of real wildness.

We met in Denver after weary days on cross-country busses and headed straight for Rocky Mountain National Park. The ranger suggested that we tackle Mount Copeland, a 13,000-foot monster, and we did despite a good case of altitude sickness. A few days later, we bagged Long's Peak, which at 14,200 feet was the highest summit in the Front Range, and nearly got zapped on the very summit by a ferocious thunderstorm. Crossing the Continental Divide by Trail Ridge Road, still unpaved then, we made our way to Leadville and Mount of the Holy Cross. The Elk Mountains beckoned next, rising up behind Aspen, which was just emerging from its past as a mining town. There we were entranced by the sound of classical music resounding from the decaying brick facades. We failed on Capitol Peak, but tramped over much of the wilderness surrounding the Maroon Bells in almost incessant rain. "This weather is for the clams" was Ralph's gloomy assessment. Continuing westward, we crossed Wolf Creek Pass to Durango, detoured to Mesa Verde, and then headed north to Silverton and Ouray. From there, we walked up to the high pastures of American Flats to climb the local biggies, Uncompahgre Peak and the Wetterhorn. The meadows were thick with sheep, and we camped with herders who had not seen a stranger in weeks and slaughtered a sheep to celebrate the occasion.

We hitchhiked everywhere, then illegal in Colorado, and were nailed at last by the State Patrol. Having been warned to get out of the state, we took the next bus into Utah and holed up in a railroad shed in Cisco, in company with several other bums, while yet another storm flashed and boomed outside. Lucky thumbs took us to Arches National Monument, to Zion and Bryce, and eventually to the north rim of the Grand Canyon. I shall never forget the friendly stranger who picked us up in the middle of nowhere, took us to his home in Richfield, let us camp in his backyard, and fed us breakfast. When we thanked him, he said, "Now you boys remember, Mormons do not have horns." We descended to the bottom of the Grand Canyon, then climbed up to the south rim, arriving in blazing heat on Labor Day. The San Francisco Peaks came next, and then it was time to go our separate ways.

Ralph was inducted into the Army in Flagstaff. He subsequently earned a PhD in marine biology in Florida, but settled at the University of Utah. We remained close friends until his untimely death in 1992. I carried on by thumb across the

Mojave Desert to Los Angeles (where family friends offered a civilized break) and then continued to Berkeley. A fresh and open-ended chapter then began, but another die had been cast. The West ("the land of room enough and time enough") with its dramatic landscapes and limitless spaces had laid a spell that would endure for the rest of my life.

Ruth, 1952 – Present

One of those trivial events that turns out to have large consequences occurred shortly after arriving in Berkeley. I lodged in International House, the graduate student residence, and in the cafeteria I picked up an attractive young woman whom I had already noticed in the Life Sciences Building. Ruth Catsiff was a graduate student in microbiology; originally from New York/New Jersey and Jewish. She had just graduated from the University of Arizona, which lent her a touch of the exotic and piquant. We quickly discovered common interests in hiking and camping, travel, science, and much else besides. Like me, Ruth had fallen under the spell of the West. Within a few months, we became a steady couple. We joined the hiking club and began to explore our new surroundings, often traveling by thumb. (Times really were different then.) Unwittingly, we were laying down a pattern for living that would become permanent and help keep the balance between work and pleasure. We also decided that we would remain in the West, whatever that took. I don't remember ever formally proposing to Ruth, we just came to take it for granted. And so in February 1954, we journeyed by train to New York City to be married, and sixty years later, we feel pretty confident that this marriage will last.

Lasting marriages are not made in heaven; you have to keep burnishing them. We have had our share of ups and downs but were able to work through them and come out stronger. We cherish the joy and contentment that marriage has brought. We have been full partners both in the art of living and the art of science. Ruth earned a Masters degree in microbiology and became quite famous for her re-discovery of *Leucothrix*, a marine bacterium with a most uncommon life cycle that had first been described a century earlier but was then lost again. She eventually became a member of my laboratory and provided the stable background against which all else unfolded. She will appear often in these pages, either by name or subsumed under the impersonal "we". Our daughter Lynn Stephanie was born in 1962, grew up in Denver, and eventually graduated from the University of Oregon as a teacher. We have worked long hours, but also traveled extensively and seen much of what the world has to offer. That casual encounter in the I-House cafeteria turned out to be the best thing that ever happened to me.

3: Becoming a Scientist

A student is not a vessel to be filled; he is a candle to be lit.
   —Source Unknown

Berkeley, 1952 – 1955

The University of California at Berkeley was perhaps the premier public university in the country. A decade earlier, a crisis over a state loyalty oath had decimated the humanities faculty; a decade later, the Free Speech M ovement would roil the campus. But in between, the 'fifties were a time of relative calm and contentment, of turning inward, and especially so for scientists. Science had proven its practical worth during the Second World War and was now widely respected as the basis of both economic prosperity and political power. A program of federal research grants had begun to funnel support into science, basic as well as applied, and biology became a prime beneficiary. Federal largesse would swell further when the Russians put the first satellite into orbit (1957). The United States, jolted out of its complacency, responded by expanding funding for science education as well as research, generating a tide that visibly lifted all our boats. It coincided with the dramatic transformation of biology itself, which came to be associated with the novel discipline of molecular biology. Few of us understood the magnitude of that revolution, and for certain, this freshman graduate student did not. But we students did sense the spirit of the times, the promise of science as a vocation and a way of making a living as never before, and we ran with it.

Home base was the laboratory of Professor I.L. Chaikoff in the Department of Physiology, noted for his contributions to the study of diabetes and atherosclerosis. I held a research assistantship and within days of arrival found myself immersed in experiments on the metabolism of cholesterol in rats. Radioisotopes were just becoming a major research tool. We had access to cholesterol labeled with C^{14} (synthesized in the laboratory of Professor W. Dauben in Chemistry). We injected that into rats and tracked it to learn what organs it reached and what chemical forms it assumed.

Prof. Chaikoff was not a hands-on scientist and seldom showed up in the laboratories. His forte was to manage a large group of students and postdocs (27 in my day), supported by research grants from the National Institutes of Health and other sources. To see the boss required an appointment, and to secure that you had to get past the dragon that guarded his privacy, in the form of a diminutive but fierce Japanese lady named Aiko Maeda. As an incoming student I was immediately assigned to one of the senior postdocs, Marvin Siperstein (who later achieved distinction for his own work on lipid metabolism), and I could not have wished for a better mentor. It was Marvin who taught me rat surgery, and the biochemical techniques required to separate the radioactive products of cholesterol degradation, identify them, and interpret the results. More importantly, Marvin introduced me to the practicalities of doing research, recording data, and turning numbers into a publishable paper. The road to a successful and satisfying career in research is easy enough in principle, but quite hard to follow: work, finish, publish. The craft of scientific writing was the one skill that was imparted by the boss, and an invaluable gift it is. All in all, we received very focused and down-to-earth training. Chaikoff was not an inspiring role model and was cordially disliked by most of his students. I came to hold him higher than most, probably because he was always very decent to me personally, treated my parents with respect when they visited, and because I learned early on that he bore a personal cross with stoic dignity.

My career plan at the time was to become a medical scientist, but the gods had other notions. The campus was crackling with new ideas and experimental approaches. The pathways of cellular metabolism, photosynthesis, and the nature of viruses were only a few of the mysteries that had begun to surrender their secrets. I had enrolled in an interdisciplinary program called Comparative Biochemistry that brought together biochemically oriented faculty from many departments, including physiology, biochemistry, microbiology, and even psychology. My instructors included some of the pioneers of molecular biology, particularly Arthur Pardee and Gunther Stent. And among the required courses was one on Microbial Chemistry, taught by Roger Stanier, Michael Doudoroff, and Eric Conn. Stanier was just then at the height of his powers, a productive investigator, elegant writer, and inspiring lecturer, who turned half the class onto microbiology. Of what Stanier said in his ten lectures, sixty years ago, I remember nothing. But the message that I heard resonates with me still: Microbes are the smallest and simplest living things; if you want to understand the phenomenon of life, study bacteria, not rats. The fact that Ruth, my wife to be, was a student of Stanier's undoubtedly helped and gave me personal entry into that world. I finished my thesis on the degradation of sterols to bile acids, resolved to kill no more animals in the name of science, and morphed into a microbial physiologist – quite undeterred by my total lack of qualifications in that field.

Summer Soldier, 1955-1957

I was awarded a Ph.D. in Comparative Biochemistry in June 1955, and a few months later, I found myself a private in the U.S. Army. It was my own fault. The draft was still on, and for years I had received deferments while completing my studies. It seemed sensible to get this obligation out of the way before starting a career and a family, so I volunteered for induction. How could I know that a month later President Eisenhower would waive the service requirement for men with advanced degrees? By then, the bureaucratic machine had begun to grind and could not be stopped. I resigned myself to two wasted years, but matters turned out quite otherwise.

Basic training was stressful. (I am no marksman and would have held up my whole platoon had our sergeant not fudged the test results.) However, matters improved afterwards. At that time, the Army had a number of laboratories scattered around the country prepared to make some use of draftees with technical training. I learned about the Medical Nutrition Laboratory in Denver from a previous inmate and sent a formal request (through channels) for the Commanding Officer to pull me out of the pool upon completion of basic training. It worked, and in January 1956, Ruth and I drove our ancient Chevy to Denver, by way of the Navajo Reservation and Santa Fe, NM, and I reported for duty in my handsome olive-drab dress uniform. As a married man I was allowed to live off base. Ruth landed a job at the University of Colorado School of Medicine, and we settled down to make the best of our new circumstances. We soon came to like Denver, the High Plains, and especially the ready access to the high mountains of the Front Range.

The Medical Nutrition Laboratory (affectionately known to its inmates as the Nut Lab) was a small, freestanding unit housed on the sprawling campus of Fitzsimmons Army Hospital in Aurora, CO, just east of Denver. Its mission was to improve the nutrition of soldiers, particularly to develop methods of preserving rations by x-irradiation. The scientific director and most of the staff were civilians, and I was assigned to one of them. Dr. Zygmund Ziporin was a nutritionist by training, a friendly and quite non-military man, and luck was again on my side. Zyg had wrangled a small grant from the Army to investigate the effects of radiation on bacteria, but had neither the aptitude nor the training for basic research. Such insecurities did not trouble me – why, as a freshly minted Ph.D. I knew how to do research! We quickly struck a bargain. I would work in the lab, get publishable data, and prepare a paper or two that would benefit us both. Zyg would keep the Army off my back, so that I would not waste time driving trucks and picking up cigarette butts on the lawns. We both kept our promises. As a result, I had nearly two years entirely on my own to master the craft of research while ostensibly bearing arms in the defense of my country. My military career (I rose from private to corporal) was neither glorious nor heroic, but highly educational in many ways.

One especially valuable lesson was that not all smart and capable persons hold degrees, and the converse is also true. Our unit was commanded by a colonel, a physician who had remained in the service after the war; a decent and well-meaning man, his chief aim was to retire in peace. The two majors were both alcoholics and largely dysfunctional. The man who ran the unit was Master Sergeant Di Pompeii, a bantam of a soldier just tall enough to pass Army regulations and with the minimum of formal education, but capable, ambitious, and disciplined. Sarge represented order, and being somewhat short on inches myself, he earned my utmost respect.

The science went well, remarkably so. Since the project was to center on radiation I elected to look at the effect of ultraviolet light (and of certain "radiomimetic" substances) on the synthesis of macromolecules in *Escherichia coli*, the model bacterium of the day. I had never done work of this kind before and had first to teach myself basic microbiological techniques. Having a microbiologist right at home came in very handy! The results were clear: The treatments blocked multiplication of the cells immediately, and also the synthesis of DNA, but the accumulation of proteins and RNA continued. At sufficiently low doses, the cells eventually recovered and resumed both DNA synthesis and multiplication, a process that required the prior synthesis of one or more proteins.

It was hardly a major contribution to the advancement of science, but the first that was wholly my own. The work was immediately accepted for publication and attracted some interest, including invitations to speak. It also brought me into contact with an eminent scientist, whose pet hypothesis was contradicted by my findings. Prof. Seymour Cohen, whom I visited while on leave, listened politely (he had already reached the same conclusion himself), and then offered me a position in his lab. It was a lesson in how a mature scientist handles a brash but bright young critic, and I have had occasion to apply it since.

Cal Tech, 1957-1959

Young scientists aiming for an academic career are expected to spend a few years in the laboratory of an established investigator, acquiring experience and becoming naturalized in the profession. With the date of my discharge from the Army approaching, I secured a postdoctoral fellowship from the National Institutes of Health and a place in the Biology Division of the California Institute of Technology. I had become fascinated with biochemical genetics (broadly speaking, how genes determine and affect the biochemical activities of living things); Cal Tech was a hub of research in this field and a good jumping-off place for academic employment. In early fall, we drove our old Chevy, by now somewhat decrepit, back across the Southwest, nursing it from one mechanic to another (it chose to die right on the bridge across the Colorado River in Yuma), and at last made it to Pasadena. We were put off by the endless sprawl, the acrid smog and the traffic, but Southern California was the choice we had made. Ruth found a good job in the laboratory of a prominent fungal geneticist, and we turned the page.

Cal Tech, even more than Berkeley a few years earlier, was crackling with excitement. The guru of the molecular biology movement, Max Delbrück, had taken up residence there.

Several of the most illuminating experiments in the field were carried out in the Biology Division, using novel techniques developed in-house. I wish I could claim that I appreciated the significance of all that was happening, but in truth my focus was on less lofty matters. Under the guidance of Hershel K. Mitchell, a distinguished geneticist renowned for his work with the bread mold *Neurospora crassa*, I began to look into an odd corner of biochemical genetics. Earlier investigations had turned up the curious fact that mutants *of Neurospora* deficient in the synthesis of amino acids and other metabolites commonly accumulated large amounts of inorganic polyphosphate, a macromolecule made up of long chains of phosphoryl groups.

What was that about? Polyphosphates had intrigued me ever since they cropped up on my qualifying examination at Berkeley, particularly the hint that they might serve as a reservoir of biological energy (as another phosphoryl molecule does in muscle). At the time, not much was known about polyphosphates: How are they synthesized and broken down? Why do they sometimes accumulate? And what function do they serve? Here was an almost virgin field, and I set to it with a will. In the course of two years, I began to gain some insight into these matters and garnered evidence that polyphosphates store phosphate but not energy. Nothing earthshaking, but respectable enough to seek an academic job.

My first attempts to pass myself off as a microbial physiologist were unsuccessful. Anxiety was beginning to set in when a letter arrived from Zygmund Ziporin, my supervisor in the Army, alerting me to a position in a newly formed research unit at the National Jewish Hospital in Denver. I applied, flew out to be interviewed, and was offered the post. A hospital that had little standing in academe was not what I had in mind, but in the end the lure of the Rockies overcame our doubts. I accepted the offer, intending to remain until an academic opportunity presented itself, and wound up staying for 30 years. Without fully realizing it, I had come to the place where the roads divide and chosen the one less traveled by. I still wonder how much of a difference that choice made.

4: Worlds to Conquer

History will be kind to me, for I intend to write it.
  —Winston Churchill

With the move to a professional research position, my formal education came to an end. But research, like painting or skiing, is an art that is only mastered by doing. For a scientist, it entails long hours in the lab, endless reading, papers to publish and grants to win, students to train, and participation in the administrative and institutional tasks that keep the wheels turning. Education continues indefinitely. Most of us find the academic life immensely rewarding and would not trade it for any other, but the details make tedious writing and soporific reading. Let this chapter serve, for the record, as a brief synopsis of a lifetime in research.

National Jewish, 1959-1989

The National Jewish Hospital was a distinctly offbeat institution, and to some degree, remains so today (current name,

National Jewish Health). Founded in the latter part of the 19th century as a tuberculosis sanatorium, diseases of the chest were still its primary focus. Patients came to National Jewish from all across the country, with one thing in common – none could afford to pay for their care. NJH was free, charity-supported (chiefly by the Jewish community of the East Coast), and almost painfully non-sectarian. Unlike most hospitals, it was also hospitable to basic science. The Director of Research, Gardner Middlebrook, was a physician who pioneered the development of protocols for treating tuberculosis with isoniazid; that new drug would revolutionize public health and bring about the closure of almost all sanatoria. He was also a man of great charm and wide interests, and he was confident that advances in basic understanding would generate progress in clinical medicine. (Few yet understood that, although the principle is quite correct, the road from the laboratory bench to the bedside is lengthy, rocky, and slow). The Neustadt Research Building had just been opened, and I was a founding member of the new Division of Research, in charge of my own laboratory and program. The lab was quite empty except for a tabletop centrifuge, and a young woman who introduced herself as my new technician and wanted to know what she could do today.

We soon got the lab up and running, and the first experiments under way. Within the next couple of years, I arranged for an adjunct faculty position in Microbiology at the University of Colorado School of Medicine, just a few blocks away, and with it the opportunity to participate in teaching. I also acquired my first research grant, the coveted RO1 from the National Institutes of Health. That was considered optional, but since the money was available, we felt that we should take advantage of it.

(That relaxed attitude seems downright unbelievable in the light of today's circumstances and was soon to change). Ruth joined the laboratory, initially as a volunteer so as to avoid even the appearance of nepotism. We were careful never to share office space and managed to avoid other potential sources of conflict. For the next 30 years, she carried out her own projects within the common program and provided continuity to the technicians, postdocs, and students that passed through our doors.

Do whatever you want to do, Gardner had told me, and I took him at his word. I continued to work on polyphosphates, but with the bacterium *Aerobacter* (now *Klebsiella*) *aerogenes*, which accumulates huge amounts of polyphosphate, rather than a fungus. Between 1961 and 1963, Ruth and I isolated a set of mutants defective in various aspects of polyphosphate metabolism and used them to clarify the synthesis, breakdown, and regulation of this class of molecules. The work produced a string of research papers and generated the concept of a polyphosphate cycle: synthesis by the transfer of phosphoryl groups from adenosine triphosphate (ATP) to the growing chain, and breakdown by hydrolysis mediated by polyphosphatase. The cycle is part of an elaborate network of reactions that regulate the economy of inorganic phosphate, a key cell metabolite, but has nothing to do with energy storage. More recent research by others has implicated polyphosphates in a number of cellular processes, but our essential conclusion still stands. I summarized the field in a major review article (Harold, 1966), which is still cited occasionally, and learned that I enjoy writing even better than benchwork.

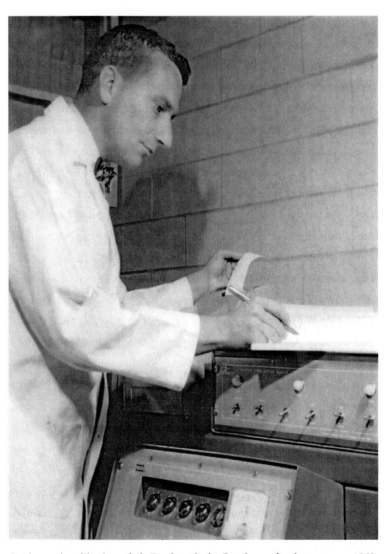

Bright-eyed and bushy-tailed: Frank with the Raytheon planchet counter, 1963.
National Jewish photo, photographer unknown.

A serious business, science! Ruth in the lab, 1963. National Jewish photo, photographer unknown.

When it became clear that polyphosphates are not central to the workings of cells, I cast around for a weightier subject. The choice fell on the transport of nutrients across the plasma membrane of bacteria, especially the movement of inorganic ions such as potassium and sodium. That line of inquiry flourished prodigiously after 1967, for it led directly into one of the most fundamental and most contentious issues in cell physiology, the molecular nature of "energy transduction". Briefly, it was known that a compound called adenosine triphosphate (ATP for short) serves as the main cellular energy currency. Like money, ATP is expended for the acquisition of goods and services, such as the synthesis of cell substance and motility. Cells consume lots of ATP, millions of molecules in each generation, and we knew that the function of the great highways of metabolism, including respiration and photosynthesis, is to continuously replenish that ATP. We also knew the enzyme that actually produces ATP, a complex protein associated with cellular membranes, dubbed ATP synthase. What was totally unclear was how the energy released by the major metabolic highways is captured and harnessed to the production of ATP. It seemed to have something to do with an "energized state" of the membrane that bears the ATP synthase, and that elusive state also provided the driving force for much of the uptake of cellular nutrients. I never intended to dive into this mess, but stumbled into it almost by accident.

Figure 4.1

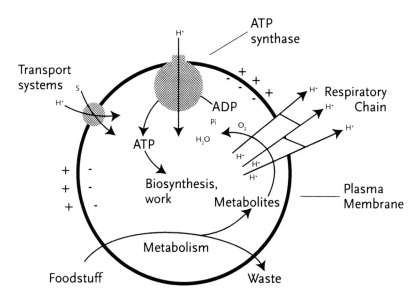

Chemiosmotic energy coupling in principle. The diagram depicts an abstract bacterial cell that lives, as we do, by respiration: it oxidizes organic substances with oxygen as the oxidant. A major product of this oxidation is ATP, the universal energy currency of all living things, which supports biosynthesis and other kinds of work. 'Oxidative phosphorylation' is inextricably linked to cellular membranes, in this instance the plasma membrane. The respiratory chain, a cascade of enzymes that funnels electrons from various metabolites to oxygen, is built into and across the membrane such that respiration pumps protons from the cell's cytoplasm into the external medium. Since the membrane is intrinsically impermeable, this generates an electrical gradient (interior negative) that pulls the protons back home. But they can only cross the membrane by specific routes, one of which is the ATP synthase, a rotary engine that uses the flux of protons to generate ATP. Other devices that allow the passage of protons are various transport systems, which use the flow of protons to pump nutrients into the cell. The diagram shows a single ensemble of each kind, but in reality the membrane is studded with hundreds of them.

A radically novel hypothesis, formulated in 1961 by a somewhat eccentric English scientist named Peter Mitchell, claimed to solve the problem: The linkage between respiration and the ATP synthase is not chemical at all, as everyone supposed, but electrical! The key is a current of protons, hydrogen ions carrying a positive charge, across the membrane that bears the ATP synthase; this current, normally generated by the respiratory chain or by the photosynthetic apparatus, drives ATP production (Fig. 4.1). The proton current also drives certain transport processes, including the transport of ions. At the time, few understood Mitchell's "Chemiosmotic Hypothesis", and fewer still took it seriously. I had to, since my own experiments began to suggest that, daft or not, he was somehow on the right track.

I had chosen to work with a bacterium called *Streptococcus faecium* (now called *Enterococcus hirae*) that lacks both respiration and photosynthesis and generates all of its ATP by glycolysis, a metabolic pathway well understood from work with animal cells. That made "Strep" singularly convenient as a vehicle to explore the linkage between metabolism and nutrient uptake. Oddly, my colleague Adolf Abrams had found that this organism contains massive amounts of the ATP synthase, even though there was no obvious use for it. Moreover, while following up on a recent paper by Allan Hamilton of the University of Aberdeen in Scotland, we noted that certain antimicrobial agents known to dissociate respiration from ATP synthesis ("uncouplers") also block nutrient accumulation by Strep, even though that organism has no respiration to uncouple! This made no sense – unless Mitchell's musings were correct.

Figure 4.2

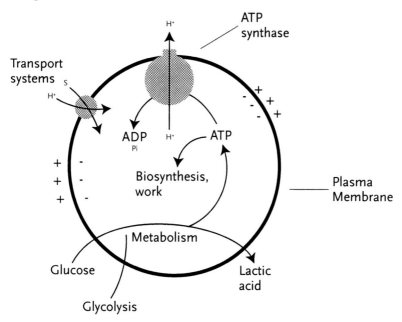

The chemiosmotic *Streptococcus*. 'Strep' does not utilize oxygen. It lacks a respiratory chain and makes its living by fermenting glucose to lactic acid. The enzymes of this pathway are free in the cytoplasm, not bound to the membrane, and produce ATP directly. In this organism the ATP synthase operates in reverse, as an ATPase: ATP is hydrolyzed to ADP and inorganic phosphate, and protons are pumped out of the cell. This generates an electrical potential which, in turn, energizes the uptake of nutrients and other kinds of work.

For several weeks in 1967, I stayed home with a sheaf of Mitchell's publications and my slide rule. I derived the equations for myself, struggled mightily with the underlying physical chemistry (never my strong suit), and one day the light went on. It was almost a physical sensation of enlightenment, a little "satori", and one of the most exhilarating experiences science has to offer. I have had several such moments since, but never again so intense as the first. Suddenly all of bioenergetics came together to make sense. The mysterious "energized state" of a membrane is none other than the current of protons across it. Thus, the function of the ATP synthase in an organism such as Strep is not to use that current to produce ATP, but rather to work in reverse, generating the current by consuming ATP (Fig 4.2). I was left in no doubt whatever that the weird, almost dreamy chemiosmotic hypothesis was true in principle. The new paradigm put me well outside the main stream of biochemical thought, but at the leading edge of a tiny movement that would in time overturn the established framework of bioenergetics.

I returned to the lab with a renewed sense of purpose: to test and verify the hypothesis by experiment and to explore its application to various aspects of bacterial physiology. That goal was far removed from the aims of a charity-supported hospital dedicated to diseases of the chest, but an appreciation of basic academic research would be part of the institutional soul for another two decades, and has not altogether faded even now. By 1967, we had a Division of Cellular and Molecular Biology, a small but quite select unit closely associated with the University of Colorado School of Medicine. Gardner Middlebrook, who had fallen foul of the Board of Trustees, was eventually replaced by Howard V. Rickenberg, a respected basic microbiologist interested in molecular biology and its ramifications. "HVR" liked to describe himself as an anarchist, but operated as a benevolent autocrat who took upon himself most of the burdens of administration and politics. That suited me just fine, and we became lifelong friends. We took pride in our ability to attract funds from the National Institutes of Health and the National

Science Foundation, which minimized our reliance on the hospital's charity base. As a private institution, we had greater flexibility to select our colleagues than public universities do and could offer initial positions to aspiring young scientists, several of whom went on to prominent careers.

To be sure, National Jewish was an oddity, a crack in the system, but it is also true that the spirit of the times was different then. What strikes me most forcibly is that research half a century ago operated on a much smaller scale than today. Research groups were smaller and more personal, equipment was elementary, and so costs and budgets were more modest. There were no computers, no mega-data projects, and no research papers with a hundred authors. In part for that reason, scientists were allowed more freedom to follow their individual bent even if it led into the wilderness. Eccentricity was tolerated, given liberty to roam, even a little public money, and there was little pressure to justify our exploratory rambles by spelling out their relevance to societal needs.

Battle Ribbons, 1967-1985

With the focus now firmly on the coupling of metabolic energy to useful work, such as the transport of nutrients and waste products into and out of bacterial cells, my modest laboratory found a role on a much grander stage. The chemiosmotic hypothesis (theory, by now) was gratifyingly rich in predictions that could be tested in the laboratory, and that is what we set out to do. A succession of excellent postdocs joined the lab and made the work their own.[1] In the course of the next two decades, our experiments helped to clarify the effects of ionophores, a class of antibiotics and related substances that ferry ions across biological membranes. We documented that the ATP synthase, a major membrane protein, functions as a proton pump; developed methods for measuring pH gradients and electrical potentials across the plasma membrane; and demonstrated that endogenous as well as artificial ion gradients drive active transport and the rotation of flagella. Many transport processes are linked to the proton circulation, but not all: We also discovered several additional ATPases responsible for the accumulation of potassium and the expulsion of sodium and calcium.

Research on energy coupling was also proceeding in other laboratories scattered around the world – in Western Europe, the United States, the Soviet Union, and Japan. It was not long before we became embroiled in the controversies that began to swirl around Mitchell's chemiosmotic theory, known among veterans as the chemiosmotic wars (roughly 1961 to 1975). The big guns engaged over ATP generation in the powerhouses of complex cells, the mitochondria and chloroplasts. Among microbiologists, the key issue was the transport of metabolites across the plasma membrane: Is it directly, chemically linked to metabolic processes (the prevailing view) or is it driven indirectly by a proton current (as chemiosmoticists maintained)? Our most vociferous and productive antagonist was Ronald Kaback (then of the Roche Institute), and for a couple of years, Kaback and I carried on a vigorous debate both in public and in private, which left my head unbowed but distinctly bloodied.

1 Karlheinz Altendorf, Evert Bakker, Don Heefner, Hajime Hirata, Yoshimi Kakinuma, Hiroshi Kobayashi, Emilie Pavlasova, and Jennifer Van Brunt

The issue came to a head at a meeting of the New York Academy of Sciences in 1973. I was invited to stand in for Peter Mitchell, who was unable to attend. A month before the conference, Kaback sent me a preprint of a forthcoming paper, purporting to prove conclusively that the chemiosmotic interpretation of active transport was untenable. As soon as I looked at the paper, I spotted a serious technical flaw that rendered the results invalid. What to do? The right thing would be to telephone Kaback and point out the error, but that would take all the wind out of the sails of my postdocs, Karlheinz Altendorf and Hajime Hirata, who had spent long hours doing the critical experiments correctly and had confirmed the chemiosmotic predictions. So I did nothing and let matters take their course. As luck would have it, Kaback spoke first and I followed. In biblical fashion, I smote him hip and thigh; it was not pretty but it had to be done, and it settled the argument. Let me add that Kaback soon rose from defeat: Having failed to lick us, he joined us and made his conversion the foundation of an extremely successful program of research.

My growing conviction that a circulation of protons across the plasma membrane underlies energy coupling and the performance of much of the cell's work gave rise to a series of literature reviews that were designed to explain and expound the chemiosmotic viewpoint (e.g. Harold 1972, 1977, 1996). They were widely read, and I would like to believe that these articles, reinforcing the experimental work but addressed to a broad audience, helped pave the way for the general acceptance of the theory, signaled at last by the award of the Nobel Prize to Mitchell in 1978. These efforts culminated in a book that surveyed bioenergetics as a whole: *The Vital Force – A Study of Bioenergetics* was published by W.H. Freeman in 1986.

These were heady years, surely the summit of my professional life. We were fully aware that we were making a revolution in Thomas Kuhn's sense, driving a shift from one paradigm to another. To apply chemiosmotic theory you first had to "get it", to master its Zen. I traveled extensively, presenting seminars and attending meetings, and repeatedly went out to England to confer with Peter Mitchell at his private laboratory in the wilds of Cornwall and imbibe the correct doctrine from its very source. (I shall have more to say about Mitchell and chemiosmotics in Chapter 5.) He had posted a map of the world in his office, with a red pin for each of his supporters. In the early years there was but a single pin in all of the North American continent, in Denver, CO; I took great pride in that pin! Academic recognition followed, including ascent of the academic ladder, tenure, service on a number of editorial boards and grant-review panels, an honorary doctorate from the University of Osnabrück in Germany, and election to the American Academy of Microbiology. Money was always tight, but I managed to keep the laboratory continuously funded for 35 years.

From Bioenergetics to Morphogenesis, 1980–1995

By 1980, I had concluded that the chemiosmotic lode was approaching exhaustion, at least as far as my own interests went. The problem of energy coupling had been solved in principle. Further progress would call for detailed research at the level of molecular structure and mechanisms, and I had no stomach for that commitment. The restless search for fresh wilderness to explore led into an out-of-the-way corner of biology, transcellular electric currents.

Inspiration came from a bold and charismatic cell biologist, Lionel Jaffe, then at Purdue University. In the 'seventies, Jaffe showed that eukaryotic cells and organisms commonly drive electric currents through themselves. (These are not bacteria, but the large, nucleated eukaryotic cells that make up protozoa, fungi, and all higher organisms, including ourselves.) Electric current (by definition, positive charges) leaves from one region of the cell and enters at another, typically a locus of growth or development. That suggested to Jaffe that electric currents might be involved in the spatial localization of these activities. I was intrigued and eventually seduced: Could currents open a door into an untraveled hinterland – how cells grow and shape themselves?

Morphogenesis, the production of form, is a conspicuous feature at all levels of biology. It has attracted thinkers for centuries, but remains elusive to this day. Every cell and organism displays a characteristic form; more precisely, it passes through a characteristic succession of forms in the course of its life cycle. Form is inherited, but is not directly specified by any genes. Instead, form is an expression of the workings of a dauntingly complex system. Even the simplest cell is made up of millions of molecules that operate in a coordinated manner to realize every cell's purpose in life: to make two where there was just one before. To accomplish this, the molecules of life must have particular chemical properties that are broadly specified by genes; and many of them must also have a particular location in space. How do molecules know where to go, and how do they get there? This is where electric currents might come in.

One cannot do experiments on morphogenesis in the abstract; you need a particular organism to focus on. After some flailing, we settled on a well-defined subject: apical growth in fungal hyphae. Briefly, most fungi grow as long, narrow filaments called hyphae, which extend solely at the tip, or apex. They do this by ferrying secretory vesicles, manufactured and packaged along the hyphal trunk, to the tip where they are discharged. These vesicles supply precursors and enzymes for the synthesis of fresh membrane and cell wall, which are deposited exclusively at the very apex. The hypothesis predicted that fungal hyphae would generate a transcellular electric current, which plays a causal role in the localization of secretion.

Lionel Jaffe, himself a skillful biophysicist and instrument maker, had devised an ultrasensitive voltmeter called the "vibrating probe" to map the minuscule electric currents in the medium surrounding growing cells. Construction of this apparatus demanded far more technological skill than I possessed, so the inquiry hung on collaboration with a colleague and professional electrophysiologist, initially Kenneth Robinson and later John H. Caldwell. We chose to work with the water mold *Achlya bisexualis*, a rather obscure "honorary" fungus whose great virtue is that its hyphae are wide enough to be mapped with the vibrating probe and also to be punctured with conventional intracellular microelectrodes. So we built a probe and got the bugs out. (The first version was quite tetchy. I commandeered a janitor's closet, ran hot water out of the tap to keep the atmosphere saturated with steam, and Ken's technician Bob Stump and I sat in there in our underwear, gingerly moving the probe around the cells with a micromanipulator. Fortunately, later models were more stable.)

We were again fortunate in our postdocs,[2] who made the work possible. We demonstrated that *Achlya* hyphae do drive a current through themselves, which is carried by protons (hydrogen ions with a positive charge). Protons are expelled from the hyphal trunk by a proton-translocating ATPase and return into the apical region by co-transport with nutrients. The current imposes a substantial electric field across the cytoplasm, with the apex relatively positive, just as the hypothesis predicted. Nevertheless, detailed studies convinced us that the transcellular electric current is not the cause of polarized extension, but rather a consequence of the spatial separation of transport systems brought about by that mode of growth. What matters is not the flux of charge but the chemical nature of the ions that carry the current, particularly the influx of protons and calcium ions into the apex.

The manner in which growing hyphae localizes secretion to the apex has turned out to be a very complex business, that is far from fully understood. The key, it appears, is the architecture of the "cytoskeleton", a web of fibers that ramify throughout the cytoplasm and serve several essential functions. One function is to funnel secretory vesicles to the hyphal tip. Specific channels located at the apex allow calcium to enter just there. This marks the tip and supplies one of the signals that ensure the correct positioning of the cytoskeleton. The influx of protons into the tip is probably a second signal of this kind. In addition, the cytoskeleton brings directed mechanical force to bear on the tip, pressing it forward. This force supplements the undirected (scalar) force of turgor pressure, which drives general expansion.

2 Chung-Won Cho, Neil Gow, Darryl Kropf, Jan Schmid, Willie Schreurs, Yuko Takeuchi, and later Nick Money

No, it's not simple, and just how all this molecular busyness generates the characteristic shape of a hyphal tip calls for yet another layer of complexity. Our studies generated another string of technical papers and also a crop of review articles designed to expound our emerging understanding of apical growth and place it in the context of morphogenesis in general (Harold 1990, 1995, 1997, 2002, 2005).

Once again, I found myself well outside the mainstream. Biology today is intensely focused on the molecules of life and particularly on the genes that specify their structures and functions. Morphogenesis, an output of the living system as a whole, calls for a different mindset that puts cells rather than genes in the center. Living things are dynamic systems made up of innumerable molecules that draw matter and energy into themselves, maintain their identity in spite of turnover, and reproduce their own kind. All their mechanisms are molecular, but it is spatial organization that brings molecules to life. This is the theme explored in recent reviews (Harold 1990, 1995, 2001, 2002, 2005), and also in two books: *The Way of the Cell: Molecules, Organisms and the Order of Life* (Oxford University Press, 2001) and *In Search of Cell History: The Evolution of Life's Building Blocks* (University of Chicago Press, 2014). My efforts to persuade others have not been noticeably successful, but I persist in the belief that if you keep reiterating the obvious, common sense will eventually prevail.

Transitions, 1987–2000

For three decades, the National Jewish Hospital and Research Center provided a sheltered environment in which I could pursue my own bent with minimal distractions. That crack in the system closed in 1987, when Howard Rickenberg (Head of the Department of Molecular and Cellular Biology) reached the age of administrative retirement. The Board of Trustees decided to abolish the department and close out the kind of academic research in which we were engaged. Thanks to tenure I could have remained in place, but chose to seek a more congenial habitat. I presided over the dissolution of our department and then decamped for Colorado State University in Fort Collins.

In July 1989, in the midst of a ferocious heat wave, we moved the lab (5 persons including Ruth and myself, plus a truck-load of equipment and stuff) to our new home in the Department of Biochemistry and Molecular Biology. Colorado State had long since outgrown its roots as an "aggie" school to mature into Colorado's second university, but it still emphasized earthy subjects including engineering, veterinary medicine, and science. The state legislature always appreciated that, but in the eyes of the world, we ranked second to the more celebrated university in Boulder.

Once we adjusted to our new circumstances, Fort Collins and Colorado State made a most agreeable setting. I held a position as Research Professor, funded with contributions from the university, a severance package from National Jewish, and my own research grants. For the first time, I had a significant teaching obligation: an outreach course entitled "Cells, Genes, and Molecules", addressed specifically to undergraduates majoring in non-science subjects. My new colleagues tolerated my eccentricities and allowed me to round out the working years and well beyond. The laboratory program continued, but my personal participation diminished as writing consumed more and more of my time and energy.

It had long been my plan to retire at 65, and that intention was reinforced by the hunch that an application for renewal of my research grant would be turned down. By the end of 1994, the last postdoc, Nick Money, was out of the nest, and Ruth and I shut down the lab. A month later, we were on our way to Aberdeen, Scotland, for a final sabbatical abroad. Ruth worked at the bench to put our last research paper into publishable shape, while I struggled with *The Way of the Cell*.

At home in Edmonds, WA, 2001. Photo Ruth Harold

Fort Collins remained our base for another five years of writing, teaching, and reflection. In 2000, we regretfully left Colorado after 41 years, moving to the Seattle area in order to be closer to our daughter (Lynn) Stephanie, who is settled in Southeast Alaska with her own family. Stephanie married a fellow-teacher, a gifted redhead of Scottish descent named Ben McLuckie. They spent three years in the Philippines with the Peace Corps and then moved to rural Alaska to kayak wilderness waters, ski the back-country, and work like slaves teaching high school. Hoonah is a part-native village on a large wild island 45 miles west of Juneau. Some cruise ships stop there to show their clients the real Alaska, and so it is, in every respect. Stephanie teaches English and Spanish, Ben science and technology, and between the two of them they make up half the high-school faculty. Stephanie and Ben have a charming daughter of their own, who has just graduated from that high school and is starting college.

Now fully retired, I remain engaged with science as a scholar, writer, adjunct professor at the University of Washington, and philosopher without license. Ruth has taken a longer leap. Science alone never quite satisfied her creative urges. She experimented with pottery and in retirement has taken up watercolor painting in a serious way, first botanical illustration and now landscapes.

So now the work is done, and its worth and meaning are for others to judge. I have made no earthshaking discoveries, won no prizes or public acclaim, and produced nothing of practical value. What I have done, as basic scientists strive to do, is to make a constructive contribution to the global conversation of science and to attain some measure of insight into that great mystery, the nature and origin of life. We are not like painters whose works hang in museums, forever identified with the name of the individual artist. Scientists are likely to be forgotten within a decade of their retirement or death. The way of science is for the best of our achievements to endure in substance but lose their individuality, like raindrops falling into a pond. So let it be.

5: Eccentric, with a Touch of Genius

The scientific mind does not so much provide the right answers as ask the right questions.
  —Claude Levi-Strauss

Scientists generally take little interest in the history of discovery. The truth, we hold, is out there, and it matters little who first stumbles across it; if Watson and Crick had not worked out the structure of DNA, someone else would have. But the most profound insights into nature often have a personal quality that makes them akin to works of art, and the chemiosmotic theory is a case in point. Besides, of all the scientists I have ever met, it was Mitchell who made the deepest impression and who transformed my own thinking.

One of a Kind

Peter Mitchell (1920-1992) was in many ways a throwback to an earlier era, as much 19th century as 20th. His student years in Cambridge were rocky at times, but he impressed tutors and associates with the force of his intellect and came under the influence of two inspirational mentors: the microbiologist Marjory Stephenson and the membrane chemist James Danielli. By the 1950s, Mitchell had begun to grope his way out of classical enzyme-centered biochemistry towards a more holistic conception of the cell as an organized, spatially structured network of chemical reactions integrated by the plasma membrane. He was coming to see cellular membranes not as semipermeable barriers, but as foci of diverse processes centered on transport and energy production.

In 1955, Mitchell landed an appointment in the Zoology Department at the University of Edinburg, and it was there that the principles of chemiosmotic coupling first crystallized. The initial formulation (1961) was exceedingly obscure, and also not quite right. In the absence of pertinent evidence, Mitchell had to make arbitrary choices about polarity, and those proved mistaken. But all the essential elements were there: vectorial reactions set in an impermeable membrane, proton translocation, the proton-motive force, and the place of the ATP synthase.

The hypothesis was all but unanimously rejected by the leading lights of the day, which must have contributed to the mounting stress. Mitchell developed life-threatening ulcers, which induced him to abandon Scotland's harsh climate and academic life in general in favor of a rural retreat in southern Cornwall. With the help of family funds, he purchased Glynn House, a decaying manor near the small town of Bodmin and turned it into a private research institute. At the time, Glynn House consisted of little more than a dignified stone façade built around 1800, with a pile of rotting timber behind.

Mitchell rebuilt it with the use of local labor to his own design, with two wings. One was the home of the Mitchell family, with six children – some his, some hers, and some theirs. The other wing was the Glynn Research Institute, which opened in 1964 with two co-directors – Peter Mitchell and his friend and fellow-student Jennifer Moyle. In this calm and verdant setting, with a view that ranged over rolling green hills to the channel coast, Mitchell recovered his strength and put his ideas in order. Before long, anyone with a serious interest in bioenergetics would find it necessary to take the 5-hour train journey from London to engage the Wizard of Bodmin in his eyrie.

I shall never forget my own first visit in 1971. Mitchell picked me up at the station and drove me up to Glynn House. A handsome barefoot woman was introduced as his wife Helen, and he added, "…and this is our illegitimate son." The ice of formality did not last long after that, and we sat up late into the night talking about science and religion. My own findings had already convinced me that Mitchell was on the right track; by the end of that evening, I knew that I had found my Master.

The Glynn Research Institute harked back to a time when scientists were also scholars and gentlemen. Early on, Mitchell acquired the adjacent farmland, complete with a herd of cows and a manager to look after them. He was also keenly interested in the preservation of local traditions and amenities; he would purchase old Cornish cottages, refurbish them, and sell them to like-minded buyers. At one time, incensed by the continuing inflation of the currency, he began to pay his staff with home-minted coinage, the silver Glynn. Local merchants accepted them, but the venture attracted the attention of the Inland Revenue Service, which put a stop to this infringement on the prerogatives of Her Majesty's Government. Funding for the Institute was always precarious and consumed too much of Mitchell's time and energy. Besides, his health was never robust, and he grew increasingly deaf. Despite the distractions, he found time to revise and rectify his formulation of energy coupling by proton currents. The second version, a great improvement on the initial one, was enshrined in two private publications, the "little grey books" that are still treasured by Mitchell's disciples, and also in the definitive statement of the hypothesis in the *Biological Reviews of the Cambridge Philosophical Society* (1966).

Peter Mitchell. Reproduced from Biochemical Society Transactions 4: 399 – 430, 1976, courtesy of the Biochemical Society and Portland Press.

Mitchell was fully aware that the fate of his theory would hinge on experimental evidence, of which there was as yet none. This became the province of Jennifer Moyle, a skillful and patient laboratory investigator, who pioneered the painstaking measurements of pH changes and other quantities required to put flesh on the bones of theory. Without her loyal and self-effacing commitment to Mitchell and to experimental science, Mitchell's imaginative leap would probably have ended in oblivion.

As a scientific intellectual Mitchell sparkled, shooting off ideas like firecrackers, without ever losing sight of the need to verify and to test them, even unto destruction. Himself a disciple of the Viennese philosopher Karl Popper, Mitchell believed that science advances by conjecture and refutation; theories must be so formulated as to render them open to disproof. True to this principle, the chemiosmotic hypothesis fairly bristled with propositions for supporters to verify and for critics to challenge. Indeed, most of Mitchell's molecular mechanisms have been abandoned, and even the basic numerology of proton translocation by the respiratory chain and ATP synthase had to be revised. But he got the central principle supremely right: a circulation of ions (commonly protons but in some instances sodium) drives ATP generation in oxidative phosphorylation and photosynthesis and also many transport carriers; the ATP synthase, a proton-driven machine oriented across the membrane, links membrane processes to the metabolic activities of the cytoplasm. The award of the Nobel Prize in chemistry in 1978 to Peter Mitchell alone recognized the unique contributions of a singular thinker, and his long and solitary struggle for acceptance.

In 1990, we celebrated the 25th anniversary of the Glynn Research Institute with a gala occasion. By then Mitchell knew that he had incurable bone cancer, but most of us who were present did not. He passed away in 1992, and the Institute did not long survive him. But by then his work was done, and his place in biological thought secure. Mitchell was far from infallible, either as a scientist or as a man; but he was one of the thinkers who shaped biology in our time. Greatness, in my view, is not primarily a matter of technical proficiency or even important discoveries. It requires original insights that integrate the fragmentary information supplied by research into a new, broad, and comprehensible pattern. In a nutshell, it is about making the world intelligible. From this standpoint, Peter Mitchell had few peers.

The Unfinished Revolution

If you look up energy coupling in a current textbook of biochemistry or cell biology, you are sure to find it in the context of ATP synthesis by respiration or photosynthesis. The role of a proton current in these key processes is now all but universally accepted, and interest has shifted to the molecular mechanisms of the respiratory chain, the photosynthetic apparatus, and the ATP synthase. The last of these revealed something quite unexpected, a rotary machine on the molecular scale. Briefly, the flux of protons through the membrane-spanning basal piece of the ATP synthase powers the rotary motion of a shaft. This, in turn, forces the subunits of the catalytic headpiece through a cycle of configurations that generate ATP. In the transport area also, the emphasis is all on just how ion movements are coupled to the movement of substrates. More cellular aspects are, of course, known to people who work in the field but seldom appear in textbooks. The network of ionic currents that link membranes and cytoplasm into an integrated unit, which is the core of chemiosmotic thinking, commands little interest today.

This development is part of a larger trend in contemporary bioscience. The attitude of scientists has become ever more reductionist, intensely focused on molecular structures and mechanisms and on their genetic specification. Cellular aspects are likely to be brushed aside on the unspoken premise that all the higher levels of order are just secondary phenomena that will be automatically clarified once all the molecular details are in place. Physiology, with its focus on complex systems, has been displaced by biochemistry and molecular biology. To be sure, there was a strong mechanistic streak in Mitchell's own thinking; it was the idea of directional chemical reactions that motived him and led him to formulate a variety of molecular mechanisms, most of which proved erroneous. For me, the great glory of the chemiosmotic theory always resided in its holistic, integrative approach to living systems: It revolves around the workings of an emergent whole, not around its constituent parts. And so, while energy coupling by an ion current has been assimilated into the biochemical canon, it seems to me that we have failed to look up and out through the window that Mitchell pried open.

The chemiosmotic theory has often been described as a textbook example of a scientific revolution, and many of Mitchell's followers thought of themselves in these terms. In this parsing of history, we use the freighted term "revolution" in a narrow and specific sense, that of Thomas Kuhn. In the 1960s, Kuhn, a historian and philosopher of science at the University of Chicago, developed a highly influential theory about the manner in which science grows: not solely, or even primarily, by the progressive accumulation of observations and measurements, but by the replacement of one explanatory framework by another. Such paradigm shifts, in Kuhn's terminology, make up scientific revolutions. Episodes of this kind are conspicuous in the history of physics and chemistry (think of the overthrow of the phlogiston theory by the discovery of oxygen or the displacement of Newtonian physics by relativity and quantum mechanics). They are less prevalent in biology, perhaps because theory has always been secondary to the collection of data. The chemiosmotic theory is indeed a striking instance of a paradigm shift, from direct chemical coupling to indirect linkage by an ion current. To make use of the new framework you first had to "get it" and to adopt a fresh outlook and language, and that came more easily to those endowed with a physiological mindset than to classical biochemists.

So far so good, but I believe that the meaning of the chemiosmotic revolution runs much deeper. The deep and quite unexpected insight is that the capture and utilization of biological energy are indissolubly linked to the physical structure of the cell. Energy transactions are a function of biological membranes, chiefly the plasma membrane and those of mitochondria and plastids, and can only operate in a closed vesicular system free of tears, holes, and leaks. There is no life without enclosure.

Energy sources support useful work, such as ATP synthesis or transport of nutrients, with the aid of ionic currents that have a direction in space. In fact, all enzyme-catalyzed reactions have a directional ("vectorial") quality because proteins are not spherical globs; they are intricately folded structures and inherently asymmetric. This feature is not apparent when protein molecules are in solution and free to tumble every which way; but when they are fixed to a membrane (or arrayed across it), their intrinsic asymmetry lends direction to the reactions they catalyze. Many, though not all, biochemical processes in living systems are vectorial in nature, not only those associated with membranes (think microtubule assembly, DNA replication, or protein synthesis). Life is organized in space and depends on vectorial processes.

Organisms are endlessly diverse and have discovered numerous ways to access and exploit whatever energy sources their environment offers. But all free-living cells, without any known exceptions, rely on some variation of energy transduction by ion currents. The mechanisms emphasized here, respiration and photosynthesis, are the most common and familiar, but many others have been discovered, especially in anaerobic bacteria. And all of them, without exception, possess a rotary ATP synthase, either to exploit the proton current or to generate it. The ATP synthase is one of the universals of biology (albeit with variations), just like DNA, ribosomes, and phospholipid membranes; it probably goes back to the very dawn of life.

The implications of the foregoing are profound, albeit somewhat unfashionable. Living things are not aggregates of countless molecules specified by selfish genes; they are intricately organized systems. We cannot hope to understand life so long as we ignore structures, compartments, and the direction of chemical reactions. This was probably true from the earliest stage in the evolution of life; I doubt that there ever was a time when self-replicating molecules roamed free to seek their fortune. There is nothing novel or arcane in this claim; it all but leaps to the eye. Just consider freeze-dried bacteria: Add water and a pinch of sugar, and the dust of life springs back into bloom. By contrast, once cells have been dissociated into their molecular constituents, however carefully that may be done, not all the king's horses and all the king's men can put a living cell together again. Structure is an indispensable element of the living state, and once destroyed, cannot be reconstituted; only a cell can make another cell.

In later chapters, I intend to explore some of these matters in more detail. They are unfashionable in the age of molecular genetics and Big Data, but energy, structure, and spatial direction are of vital importance to any understanding of the living state. If this view of life eventually comes to prevail, the chemiosmotic theory will be recognized as a landmark step towards making life intelligible.

6: When the Going was Good

I have seen more than I remember and remember more than I have seen.
   —Lord Curzon

The latter half of the 20th century was a golden age, not only for biological science but also for travel and much else besides. Western values and power dominated the political order; borders fell open, and air-travel brought all of the world within reach. The first to benefit were Americans, lords of the universe after World War II, but the freedom to roam soon came true for Europeans also, and now includes a growing number of Latin Americans and Asians. The horizons of middle-class folks expanded to cover Western Europe, Japan, the Middle East, then the Soviet Union, China, and even Central Asia and much of Africa. The opening of Nepal gave access to the Himalayas. Travel ceased to be the prerogative of the well-to-do or young and intrepid and became an industry, now one of the world's largest. Mass travel pried open long-sealed frontiers, but also brought mobs of cruise-ship tourists to every place within reach of the coast. My hunch is that this era may be drawing to a close, partly because of the excesses of the travel industry itself, but primarily due to the progressive erosion of peace and stability underpinned by Western dominance.

Ruth and I caught the travel fever early and made it a centerpiece of our life. If we do not quite meet Rose Macaulay's stringent definition that "a traveler is a person for whom travel is the chief object of life", we do not fall far short. We have striven to see as much of the world as we can, with focus on the mountains and centers of ancient high civilization. We have done our homework and incorporated our experiences into a view of the world. Over the past sixty years, the quest has taken us from California's Sierra Nevada all over the wild country of the Western United States, Canada, and Alaska. We have roamed widely across Europe, especially the Mediterranean basin, and through the Middle East from Afghanistan to Morocco. We have trekked in the Himalayas, wandered up and down the Indian sub-continent, and followed the Silk Road from Beijing across Central Asia to the Golden Horn. The years have slowed us down, but the passion has not been extinguished.

First Forays, 1953-1968

It all began with the mountains, to which both of us are addicted, and the enchantment of the High Sierra. There is no better exercise for body and soul than walking, and in the course of sixty years we have walked the equivalent of the earth's circumference. During the Berkeley years, 1952 to 1955, we backpacked the length of the John Muir Trail from Yosemite to Mount Whitney (skipping only the short section where the trail swings away from the mountain crest). The walking then was free and easy: no permits needed, camp wherever you wish, cook over an open fire, and not too many fellow hikers. We did not even need to carry a tent, for it never rains at night in the Sierra during July and August. Never? Well, hardly ever, and a single poncho made an emergency shelter. We could carry food for exactly seven days, with every raisin counted, and on the last day, we had to locate the cache brought in by a packer from one of the towns along the eastern base or else go hungry. We emerged from each summer's trek lean, strong, and ravenous.

The "Range of Light" cemented a pattern of taking off a full month every year, sometimes more. It is an old custom among Europeans and far more sensible than the American obsession with being in business 24/7. Time for ourselves did sometimes conflict with professional ambitions and the demands of science, but we struck a middle way that has worked for us. It is undoubtedly the call of the mountains that kept us in Colorado for more than forty years, at some cost in professional success, but with incalculable gains in satisfaction with life.

Our horizons expanded almost immediately with a trip to Mexico in the summer of 1957. Mexico was an exotic country, far more so than today, before the mega-resorts and the crowds on a guided tour. I picked up enough Spanish to get by, and we were made welcome everywhere. We traveled around by bus, stayed in the small colonial towns, and reveled in the spectacular archaeology. That first exposure was followed by others – journeys into southern Mexico including Oaxaca, Campeche, Palenque, Yucatán, and the highlands of Guatemala.

Ruth was already, and remains today, an avid consumer of culture; and she soon infected me with her passion for museums, paintings, and pottery. The irresistible magnet was Europe, beginning in 1960 with Spain, still ruled by General Franco. We started in Granada with the celebration of Corpus Christi, then wandered through Madrid, Toledo, Segovia, Avila, and the caves of Altamira (still open to tourists then), ending up in Lisbon. Spain became one of our favorite countries, to which we have returned several times. Should I ever endow a university, I shall model it on Salamanca's; as for palaces, give me the Alhambra.

A first glimpse of Italy at the end of a journey to Greece was just enough to whet the appetite, and so we returned in 1964 with our infant daughter, whom we carried about in a backpack to much public delight. We rented a car, drove it from Venice through Tuscany to Rome, and fell under the spell of that marvelous but exhausting city. Another foray took us around Sicily, learning to drive Italian style, and ending up in Malta. We have never outgrown the fascination with the Mediterranean basin, from Gibraltar to the Adriatic, the Aegean Islands, and at last Turkey. Having passed from the age of solo travel to group trips and now to cruises, that world never ceases to beckon.

An introduction to the Far East came in 1967, when we traveled to Tokyo to attend an International Congress of Biochemistry. Japan was far more inspiring than the presentations; after the congress we wandered north to Nikko, then into the Japan Alps, and fell in love with Kyoto. By 1969, we were seasoned travelers, or so we thought.

Iran, 1969/70 and 2000

One of the chief rewards of the academic life is the tradition of periodic sabbatical leave to refresh the spirit, acquire new skills, or find time to explore new directions. By 1969, I felt sufficiently settled to take a year away from the lab, and I was still young enough to believe that we scientists have a moral duty to bring the light of science to those who dwell in darkness. Coupled with our enduring fascination with the Middle East, this encouraged me to apply for a Fulbright lectureship in either Turkey or Iran. After an interminable, nail-biting wait Iran came through, and in the summer of 1969, we traveled (accompanied as usual by our daughter, then 7) via Iceland and London to Tehran. It proved to be one of the most educational (and stressful) years of our life, which gave new focus to our travels and sharpened our take on the world.

Iran in the Sixties was a different place from today, politically and even culturally. The Shah was at the height of his power and reasonably popular, at least among the middle class and the merchants. Inflation was still moderate, and the secret police not yet so oppressive as to spark popular resentment. In the U.S., we tend to see the Shah as a figure of evil, a brutal and corrupt dictator. That has never been my view: I see him as a tragic figure who strove to move his country into the modern world, while also assuring the succession of his son (then just 8 years old) and preserving the monarchy as the keystone of the nation. He failed, stymied by the relentless opposition of the clergy, the deep conservatism of Iran, and the ill will of the gods. The Islamic Republic of Iran, while continuing to vilify his memory, actually carries out many progressive projects initiated during the Shah's reign.

Our first impressions of Tehran were, to say the least, unfavorable. We suffered a bad case of culture shock: that furious and reckless traffic, all those women in black cloaks (chador) and unshaven men. What were we thinking to bring our precious little daughter to this savage place? For several days we literally sat in our hotel room and cowered. Fortunately, there were things to be done – find an apartment, bargain for a refrigerator, and find our way around this strange city. And then we had the brilliant idea to get out of Tehran for a while. We flew to Isfahan, which is to Iran what Florence is to Italy. We stayed in the Shah Abbas Hotel, Isfahan's best, made contact with an Iranian friend from the past who was by then chancellor of the university, and immersed ourselves in the architecture and culture of Iran. Within days, curiosity and admiration overcame our fears, and by the end of the year, we were quite at home in Iran.

Tehran has been described by a dyspeptic visitor as "the fag-end of the Western world." For sure, there was no trace of oriental fantasy about it. We lived in North Tehran, about a mile from the University, in a modern and well-to-do section of the city, in a pleasant apartment. We could shop at the PX in the American Embassy, but bought fresh goods locally. One could even buy pork and sausages – at Arzuman's, an Armenian butcher where all the foreign residents rubbed elbows. Lynn went to the International school and liked it; every morning she was picked up by bus and delivered home in the afternoon. People on the street wore Western clothing, though the black chador was still common enough. An enduring memory of Iran is of grandma in chador escorting her teenage granddaughter in a miniskirt. All this was quite unlike the poorer and more traditional South Tehran, centered on the vast bazaar and the grand Sepah Salah mosque, where old Iran reasserted itself.

Even up in our enclave, reminders of the cultural divide cropped up. Our apartment building came with a servant, who went out early every morning to pick up a flap of *sangak*, the delicious stone-baked bread that is a staple of daily life – provided he was adequately tipped every month. Our position in the Fulbright program came with a servant of our own, a friendly Armenian woman named Sony. She did some of the cooking, cleaned the house, looked after Lynn when we went out, and did the weekly laundry in the bathtub. She was indispensable, and since she spoke no English we had to pick up Farsi just to run the house. She also taught us a little of the minorities' anxiety-filled perspective on life in Iran. And there was the frightening occasion when Lynn's school bus home was hours late; it turned out that one of the kids had diverted the driver from his routine on the strength of his father's high rank in the military.

Our social life was narrow, restricted by our limited Farsi and the general understanding that it was risky for Iranians to get too friendly with *farangis*, but we were invited to a few formal dinner parties. They began late, with hours of conversation over nuts and fruit; dinner would be served very late, about 10 p.m., and soon afterward the party broke up. (The one time that we reciprocated with a party at our home proved a minor disaster – stupidly, we served wine and that embarrassed several of our guests.) We felt most at home in the British Institute of Persian studies, where foreigners and Iranians congregated to attend lectures and use the extensive library.

We had plenty of time to explore the city, study the language, and learn about Iran. We would not, of course, buy carpets: What, walk on the eyes of children? That resolution lasted about a month; the carpets were just too tempting. The carpet shops, all in South Tehran, were mostly owned by Jews, and we came to know several of them over endless cups of tea, while one exquisite carpet after another was rolled out for our inspection. If we saw one we liked, we took it home and lived with it for a month. Only then, would we either pay for it or exchange it for another. Hiking was all-important to us, and the Alborz Mountains that rise straight out of the city's suburbs to 14,000 feet offered ample opportunity. There were no marked recreational trails, but mule tracks led to small villages tucked deep in the ravines. They were usually poor and primitive, surrounded by stony fields, fruit trees, and poplars for timber. Tracks over the passes led from one valley to the next, deep in snow during the winter. Ruth and I did some together, but I also went out with Mike Burrell, a graduate student in Persian Studies from Scotland. That included an adventurous expedition to Alamut, the thirteenth-century Castle of the Assassins deep in the high Alborz. It was all safe enough, and we never encountered a problem.

My ostensible purpose in Iran was to teach science, but it soon became clear that the University of Tehran had no idea what to do with me. They assigned me to the School of Public Health, where I was a fish out of water. But the Director and several members spoke English, and so it worked out well enough. In the absence of any official duties, I crafted my own: a course for upper-level students and a sprinkling of younger faculty on contemporary advances in cellular and molecular biology, and a workshop on scientific writing. Iran at that time aspired to join the academic life of the West, and several of my colleagues had studied abroad. They were doing research and were keen to publish their work in Western journals. I spent many hours working with individual scientists, helping them to prepare articles for journals such as the *Biochemical Journal* and the *Israeli Journal of Medicine*. (Relations with Israel were quite cordial. There was an Israeli embassy in Tehran, and Israel traded weapons for Iranian oil.) Still, the work was insufficient to fill my time, and Ruth had even less to do. The idleness was to prove the hardest part of our year as cultural ambassadors.

Light duties and a flexible schedule left ample time to travel and learn about the extraordinary civilization of Iran. We did not drive (too risky for foreigners, who would automatically be blamed in the event of an accident), but hired cars with a chauffeur to take us out. Since none of our drivers spoke English we had to communicate in Farsi, and they became our mentors in all matters Persian: Fjodor, a handsome Assyrian Christian; Hassan, a Sunni Arab from the deep South; and Hushang, a Bakhtiari tribesman from Shiraz and a true-blooded Iranian. With them we explored the Alborz Mountains, the Caspian Shore, the edge of the Central Asian steppe, and the ancient small cities that rim the great desert, the Dasht-e-Kabir. Iran Air made possible longer journeys, some official but most private: to Tabriz in northwest Iran, to Mashad with the great shrine of the Imam Reza and its golden dome, and of course into the heart of Persian civilization that still beats in Isfahan, Yazd, and Shiraz. Over No Ruz, the New Year holiday that falls in mid-March, we decamped to India for two weeks and reveled in the world's most exotic country (despite the heat, which eventually drove us out of the plains to Srinagar and the cool mountains of Kashmir).

With our year amongst the Persians drawing to a close, we hatched plans for a fitting finale: Afghanistan. That sounds grossly irresponsible today, especially with an 8-year old in tow, but it was quite reasonable in 1970. The country was at peace, governed by its king, and welcomed tourists. Iran Air took us to Kabul, then a pleasant city of some 500,000 with a famous bazaar. We hired a car from the National Tourist Organization and set out for the ends of the earth. Our driver spoke no English but Dari, the language of Afghanistan's Tajiks, is very similar to Farsi, so we got along splendidly. A long loop took us across the Hagigak Pass into the Vale of Bamiyan, nestled deep in the Hindu Kush Mountains, where the enormous statues of Buddha had kept watch for 1500 years. Then we went to Mazar-i-Sharif with its spectacular tomb of Ali, and to Balkh, the Mother of Cities. Ayn Khanum, the Greek ruin by the Oxus River, was closed to us, but we visited Tashkurgan, the ancient temple of Surkh Kotal, and returned to Kabul via the Salang Tunnel under the ridges of the Hindu Kush. A separate excursion by air took us to Herat in Western Afghanistan, with its great Timurid buildings – the Friday Mosque, assorted mausolea, and a famous bazaar. On the Ariana Airlines flight back to Kabul, I was the only male passenger not carrying a rifle. (The traditional muzzle-loading *jezail* was *de rigeur* for Afghan gentlemen.) It made us a little queasy, but we felt reassured when the pilot came on the intercom with a thick Texas drawl.

Afghanistan remains in my memory as a place of lost content, long-since overtaken by endless war. The buildings of Herat are pockmarked with bullet holes, the bazaar burnt out, the Buddhas blown up by zealots, and the Kabul museum looted. War has transformed the entire character of the country, and no one knows what will come as American suzerainty withdraws.

We returned to Tehran, and the next day, we flew to Europe. Pan Am's flight the day before had been hijacked by Palestinian terrorists, and everyone was on edge, but all went well. That night in Geneva, we learned one final lesson: In front of our hotel was a traffic light, and when it turned red, all the cars stopped! In the West, a traffic light is a categorical imperative; in the East, it's a basis for negotiation. I don't believe that I taught much in Iran, but Oh My Lord did I ever learn!

Ruth and I returned to Iran as tourists in 2000, wiser, less buoyant, but better-heeled. In those thirty years much had happened to change the face of the country: the revolution of 1979, an Islamic Republic ruled by its clergy, a hard-fisted government plagued by corruption that maintained power by the suppression of dissent, and an assertive foreign policy opposed to that of the U.S. But there was also vast wealth fueled by oil and natural gas, which paid for visible progress in terms of roads, medical care, public education, and living standards in general. The population of Iran nearly tripled between 1970 and 2000, and that of Tehran rose from 3 million to 15. Iranians generally still admire and like Americans even though their rulers do not, and we were welcomed everywhere.

We arranged a private trip with a guide, a car, and a superb Armenian driver and planned a month-long loop out of Tehran to revisit old haunts and take in sites that we could not reach in 1969/70. We drove northwest across the Alborz Mountains to Resht on the Caspian Sea, to the great shrine of Ardebil, and on to Tabriz. An excursion took us to the medieval Armenian church of San Stefano on the Aras River, the border with Azerbaijan (bristling with armed guards). Turning south, we stopped in Marageh with its ancient tomb towers and observatory. We traversed Iranian Kurdistan, with a detour to the remote site of Takht-e-Suleiman, where the Kings of ancient Persia took the crown. Then we traveled via Hamadan to incomparable Isfahan, with its medieval Friday Mosque, acres of tilework, and grand central square. We visited Nain and reacquainted ourselves with the desert city of Yazd. Turning eastward, we passed through Kerman and Mahan to reach Bam with its imposing mud-brick castle (a few years later a massive earthquake would send those walls tumbling down). We ended up in Shiraz and Persepolis and flew back to Tehran from there. Across the country, ancient monuments were well kept up and facilities much improved, but the romance of an exotic untraveled land had dissipated.

Iran is much more than a state and regional power; it is a civilization that spread its wings over western and central Asia, from India to Turkey. The architecture, literature, and visual arts of the Muslim heartland bear the imprint of Persian genius, and what we saw and learned on that first sabbatical gave direction to our subsequent interests. The seed came to fruition twenty years later.

Australia and Southeast Asia, 1975

The years that followed were professionally successful, exceedingly busy, and stressful enough to throw me into a mid-life crisis of self-doubt. It was work that pulled me through – laboratory experiments, editorial tasks, and a review panel of the National Science Foundation. It was in the Seventies that I learned from Loren Eiseley that the true use of science is to make the world intelligible, and I have lived by that mantra ever since.

Personal turmoil was no reason to stay home. We took a journey around the North Atlantic (Iceland once more, the Faroe Islands, Shetland, Orkney, and a glimpse of Scotland); a long camping trip to the Canadian Rockies (including the Bowron Chain of Lakes in a canoe too heavy for us to portage; we made a daily good deed for a troop of Boy Scouts); and we returned to Greece and the Aegean Sea (Athens, the Peloponnesus, Cycladic Island, Ephesus, Pergamon, Bursa, and Istanbul).

And then an opportunity arose that could not be passed up: I was invited to spend a year in the Biochemistry Department of the Australian National University in Canberra, introducing chemiosmotic theory to a world-class center of bioenergetics. I persuaded National Jewish to let me go, secured funding from the National Science Foundation, and in December 1974, we set off for the Antipodes with our daughter, then 12. We traveled by Pan Am via Hawaii, American Samoa, New Zealand (where we spent two weeks trundling around the southern half of the South Island in a Morris Minor with tiny wheels), and eventually Sydney. We arrived in Canberra just after the New Year, in the midst of a heat wave and a ferocious thunderstorm.

Australians find Canberra artificial and too far from the coast, but we liked it a lot. The capital was quite a small city and still under construction – the art museum, which Ruth had been counting on, was just a hole in the ground – but there was no shortage of good entertainment by visiting artists. Ruth took up pottery and Chinese history, and we both enrolled in a class on the history of Southeast Asia; and we enjoyed the relaxed social life with colleagues and neighbors. Best of all was the birdlife: rosellas and kookaburras and galahs, and the white cockatoos that flew into town every evening at dusk. We explored the nearby hills and climbed Mt. Kosciusko, which at 7,360 feet was Australia's highest peak. I lectured at Australian National University and elsewhere, and spent some time in the laboratory, but more in the library. It was here that I first encountered Lionel Jaffe and transcellular electric currents. We found Australia pleasant and congenial, but not exciting; our ears pricked up when we learned about low airfares to Indonesia.

We flew to Bali and made our base inland in the quiet artist's village of Ubud, from which we explored the enchanting villages and Hindu temples. On Java, we homed in on Jogjakarta, close to the great Buddhist stupa of Borobudur and the Hindu temples of Prambanan. We traveled out to Malang in easternmost Java and extended the trip to include the ancient port of Malacca in Malaysia and also thriving modern Singapore.

We were so taken with Indonesia that we returned in the winter on our way home. We re-visited "Jogja" and Singapore, then made our way up the coast of Malaysia to Penang, and eventually to Bangkok. All would have been well had we not relaxed our guard! We sampled street food in Singapore and came down with a bad case of Raffle's Revenge. Ruth ended up in a hospital in Bangkok for 9 days with Giardia; my case was less severe, and Lynn shrugged off the whole disaster. When Ruth was released at last we traveled to Chiang Mai for a few days, and then started for the U.S. A week in Delhi proved to be just the ticket – cool, sunny, and dry in a marvelous old city full of ancient monuments. We stayed at the Imperial, an old luxury hotel where the Raj still lingers even to this day, and reveled in the turbaned staff and the hoopoes on the lawn. And so homeward we went at last via London, rounding the globe.

Scotland, 1981/82 and After

Lynn left for college in the fall of 1981, and two weeks later, we were on our way to Scotland for another sabbatical year. Our host was Allan Hamilton of the Department of Microbiology, with whom I had kept in touch since 1967. We could not have made a better choice. Ruth worked in the laboratory of the mycologist Graham Gooday; I was deep into *The Vital Force*, and wrote a goodly chunk of it on the dining room table of our university flat at the edge of Old Aberdeen.

Home base was Marischal College, downtown and within walking distance of the harbor, a vast rambling nineteenth-century granite pile with oddly placed rooms and staircases that led nowhere. Aberdeen is an old city but not famous; few tourists travel north beyond Edinburgh. It is a provincial city in the best sense, the heart of Buchan in northeast Scotland. It is also a prosperous one: North Sea oil comes ashore near Aberdeen, repair and maintenance of the rigs is done there, and the small airport is continually busy with traffic to and from the drilling platforms. There was no unemployment in Aberdeen. To be sure, the granite architecture is on the heavy side, frequent rain dampens the spirit, and the winter is long. But it is a very livable city, with an active cultural scene, graced by a beautiful coastline and ready access to the Grampian Mountains. We became very fond of Aberdeen and made it our second home for the next 15 years.

We returned several times for shorter stints and for another full year in 1995 following retirement. Again Ruth worked at the bench, tidying up our last research paper, while I concentrated on a series of lectures in celebration of the university's 500th birthday. One time I taught a course, and one of the graduate students, Neil Gow, spent a postdoctoral year with me in Denver. We came to know both Buchan and the Highlands, and also made Aberdeen the base for explorations much further afield – to Yugoslavia in 1981 (just prior to its violent breakup), to Nepal's Annapurna in 1986, and to Southern France and the Pyrenees in 1995. Of all our sabbatical choices, Aberdeen offered the most to both of us.

Himalayan Passages, 1983-2003

For hikers, the Himalayas are the ultimate destination – no other mountains can match them. Unfortunately, Lynn had no inclination to trek for weeks with her parents and other super-annuated folks, so we put that off until she left for college. Then, while in the UK, we arranged to join a British group for a high trek in Nepal in the fall of 1983.

We signed up for a relatively easy trek but the permit was denied, and so we were transferred to a much more challenging one headed for the base-camp of Makalu. We flew to Kathmandu, but were delayed en route when our Royal Nepal flight lost an engine and had to return to Delhi in a hurry. We got in the next day, had 30 minutes to repack, and caught the connection to Tumlingtar. The walking was on good trails but far from easy: up and down along a high ridge paralleling the Arun river, sharply down 3,000 feet to the river, across on a swaying suspension bridge, and then up and over the Barun Pass at about 14,000 feet. Ruth and I had trouble keeping up with the group and eventually made camp in a lovely meadow while the group pressed on to the foot of Makalu. On the way back, we got caught in a substantial snowfall, which made the trail quite treacherous. No one was eager to re-cross that suspension bridge, so we followed the right bank of the Arun for several days and eventually crossed it near Tumlingtar. By the end of the trek we had fallen in love with the Himalayas and the trekking life, but had to recognize that we could not keep up with younger and fitter folks. We resolved to return to the Himalayas, but on private treks so we could set the goal and speed, and factor in rest days.

In the course of the next two decades, we managed six more high treks and count these among the highlights of our travels: Everest and the Sherpa villages, 1984; Annapurna Circuit, 1986; Baralacha La and Chandra River, 1991; Langtang, 1994; Bhutan, 1996; and Sikkim Kanchenjunga, 2003. All were set up in the classic manner, with our own expedition. We had a *sirdar* in charge (I served as the "white leader"), a cook with one or two helpers, and up to 15 porters. We camped every night and were self-sufficient in food and fuel. Being well used to camping and roughing it outdoors, we reveled in the life. You walk, eat, manage your personal needs, and sleep; next day you do it again. All the cares and concerns of "normal" life fall away, and only the mountains abide. There is nothing else quite like it.

We loved every one of our treks, but the Annapurna Circuit stands out for its length (200 miles over 26 days) and the challenge of the high pass, the Thorung La, at nearly 18,000 feet. We started from Kathmandu with our own crew of 11 porters, picked up six more at the trailhead, and began walking at about 1,500 feet in the banana belt. For the next 11 days, we followed the Marsyangdi River, climbing steadily through Chame and Pisang to Braga with its fantastic monastery at about 11,000 feet. After an acclimatization halt, we continued up and further

up, through the town of Manang, to the foot of the high pass
at 14,000 feet. We did not feel fully acclimatized, but there was
nothing for it now. We rose at 2 a.m. to begin the hardest day's
walk we have ever done. We had nearly 4,000 feet to climb, one
slow step at a time, hunched over our walking sticks and stop-
ping frequently to gulp in the thin air. More than once we were
sorely tempted to give up, until we crossed a long, steep snow-
field; there was no more talk of turning back after that (our
crew strolled across in flip-flops). The weather was glorious, the
views endless. After a rest on top of the Thorung La, we started
down, took a nap at the first grassy meadow, and reached the
Hindu pilgrimage site of Muktinath at about 12,000 feet late in
the afternoon.

Pooped but proud. On top of the high pass, Thorung La (17,650 ft), on the
Annapurna circuit, Nepal, 1986.

I declared a rest-day, and then we dropped down and down into the gorge of the Kali Gandaki River. We passed through small villages and then towns – Kagbeni, Jomosom, Thukche, and Marpha (locally famed for its delicious Dal Bhat, a dish of rice with lentils), then slipped back into the foothills at Tatopani hot springs (such luxury, a wash with hot water!). But then it was up once more, across the 10,000-foot pass of Ghorepani to Poon Hill with its famous view of Dhaulagiri, and eventually to a group of high villages inhabited by Gurkhas. We detoured a little towards the Annapurna Sanctuary, but did not enter it. And so we came to trail's end at the bottom of 3,000 feet of relentless stone steps, and the fleshpots of Pokhara.

In the Eighties and Nineties, only a few roads penetrated the high mountains. People traveled on foot, and goods were carried on mule-back or by porters. Along the most popular trails simple lodges had begun to spring up; by camping with our own crew, we avoided the intestinal and respiratory illnesses that plague so many trekkers. Today the Annapurna Circuit is more popular than ever, but not nearly as otherworldly as it was even 30 years ago. You can fly to Jomosom and drive up the Marsyangdi River; only the high pass is the same as it was. We were lucky with the weather, or perhaps Lord Vishnu was in a benevolent mood. Just recently a freak snowstorm caught hundreds of hikers on the pass, killing some two dozen. Never underestimate the hills and the snows of the hills!

Silk Road, 1997-2012

In the years following the Australian sabbatical, our travels came to focus on Asia. Not exclusively, of course; we found time for summer trips into the Rocky Mountains, especially the Canadian Rockies, which became a habit, and into the canyon country of the Southwest. Mountain trips abroad included the Scottish Highlands, the Peruvian Andes, the Pyrenees, and the pilgrimage road to Santiago. We took rafts down Alaska's Copper River and kayaks into Glacier Bay, down the Stikine River and into the Sea of Cortez. Even so, it's the journeys to the Himalayas and exotic locales in Asia and the Middle East that stand out in retrospect: A winter trip to China in 1986; the Philippines in 1989, to visit Stephanie (Lynn now goes by her middle name) and Ben, followed by a return to Japan. Then in 1990, we did a marvelous journey by car across India's Deccan, from Bombay to Mysore and ultimately to the temple-city of Madurai deep in the South. We returned to India the following year, this time to Ladakh beyond the high Himalayas, a region politically in India but culturally Tibetan. In 1992, we traveled to Egypt and Israel, my first return to the land of my youth but not the last. Turkey featured several times, most notably in 1993 when we traveled to Ankara and south to the coast. We made it to Tibet in the spring of 1998, and in the fall, to Syria, Jordan, and Israel. And always in the back of the mind was the lure of Central Asia and the Silk Road, tantalizingly out of reach.

The Silk Road presently refers collectively to the network of trade routes that, in antiquity and the middle ages, linked China with India and Europe. There was never a road as such, but rather a web of caravan tracks and routes, supplemented by sea lanes. Tentacles reached out to Afghanistan, Korea, Mongolia, across the steppes, and into Russia. We had touched upon the Silk Road while living in Tehran, since a main caravan trail passed across all of northern Iran; and eventually it became a distinct project to explore as much of that trans-continental web as we could manage. In 1997, we joined a group from Wilderness Travel led by the redoubtable Roger Williams, to journey from Xian, China to Islamabad, Pakistan, with many stops in between. We passed through Lanzhou and Xining, spent a day at the Kumbum Monastery, and drove across a corner of the Tibetan plateau to the Mogao cave temples at Tun Huang. We stopped in Turfan, Urumchi, and then Kashgar for its bustling Sunday market and Id Gah mosque. Crossing the Karakorum Montains by the Khunjerab Pass, we dropped down into Hunza; traversed Swat; visited the ruins of Taxila; and at last reached Islamabad (where an earnest worshipper in the mosque did his best to convert me). Ruth and I added an extension to Lahore, broiling hot in June but at the height of the mango season. We returned home tired but satisfied and resolved to do it again.

Having discovered the merits of group travel, particularly for older travelers, that became part of the pattern; and being now retired, we had more time to travel. In 1999, we made it to Central Asia at last, traveling from Ashgabat in Turkmenistan via Khiva, Bukhara, Samarkand, Osh, and the Ferghana Valley to Tashkent. We returned to Iran in 2000 on a private trip, and also to India (Ladakh and Spiti, 2001; the deep South, 2003; Rajasthan, 2005). The destination for 2006 was Eastern Anatolia, a superb private trip with Serdar Akerdem as our guide and driver. The southern Caucasus (Armenia, Georgia, and Azerbaijan) came in 2007, with Roger. We joined him again in 2008 for an adventurous journey across the Pamirs (Urumqi, Kashgar, Khunjerab Pass, and Hunza, a corner of Kirghizstan, the Pamirs, the upper Amu Darya river, and Dushanbe), and once more in 2010 for a reprise of the caravan cities of Central Asia. We have not traveled all the Silk Road between Xian and Constantinople, but have sampled most of it. These journeys became the basis for a series of articles on historical geography published in *The Silk Road* and for a string of public lectures (jointly with Ruth) on the history and civilization of the Middle East.

So now the years are beginning to take their toll on both of us. Adventure travel is over and adaptation is the order of the day. We have reached the cruising age: Antarctica in 2013, Central America in 2014, and the Black Sea in 2015. We intend to keep on doing what it is possible to do and to keep it up as long as possible.

Journey's Harvest

Why travel, and why do it so intensely? The usual off-the-cuff answers merely brush away the question: because it's fun, because it's there, because it beats waiting passively for the hearse, it's a sublimation of the sex drive or suppresses the horror of home... It's one thing to take periodic holidays and enjoy a change of scene and quite another to roam the globe obsessively as though in search of something that always remains out of reach.

For sure, travel broadens the mind and has given us a satisfying sense of accomplishment. Thanks to our travels, we live in a wider world, whose bounds stretch far beyond the borders of the United States of America. Travel has shown us both the beauty of the world and its burdens and made us aware of the complexity and ambiguity of the tapestry that history weaves. If you still believe that the intertwined problems of economics, politics, and morality have simple solutions, you need to get out more. But an education in the world's intricate diversity, however valuable, is not the reason why one sets foot on the road that goes ever on and on. That must go deeper.

I would like to believe that the underlying impulse is the same as that which channels some people into research and keeps them there for a lifetime: a restless quest for novelty, discovery, variety. Like Tennyson's Ulysses, growing old on the shores of Ithaca and conscious of approaching mortality:

> Much have I seen and known...
> Yet all experience is an arch wherethro'
> Gleams that untravell'd world whose margin fades
> Forever and forever when I move.

Some people feel an overpowering need to roam; most do not, and that's just as well.

7: Sailing to Byzantium

... to sing to lords and ladies of Byzantium of what is past, or passing, or to come.

—W.B. Yeats

Education, it has been said, is what remains when all that was learned has been forgotten. Over the years, I have listened to countless lectures and seminars, read thousands of articles and books, and mastered a few practical skills (all now obsolete). I have also traveled extensively and seen for myself the diversity of human cultures, religions, and historical experience. Most of what I learned has long since been forgotten, but I have retained some of the substance and come away from my education with a well-defined outlook on the world. Let me here ruminate a little on what is past, or passing, or perhaps to come, in science and the world at large.

Science, for me, has supplied an overarching framework that makes good sense of the material universe, at least that portion which is accessible to our senses and instruments. Most people draw their conceptual scaffold from religion, but for some, science now takes the place of the traditional formulas. Nature, we hold, is hard to comprehend but neither capricious nor inscrutable – as long as our questions do not probe too deeply. Like others before me, I have found the quest for understanding utterly absorbing and satisfying, much more than a way to earn a living. It is a vocation, even a calling, and sometimes an obsession that rules our lives. Having said that, I am keenly aware of the limitations of science as a worldview. Science is like a game played on a board, and human affairs lie off that board. Science has nothing useful to say about right and wrong, love and hate, and how to live a decent life in a complicated and fractured world where good and evil are inextricably entangled. When it comes to the questions that matter most in daily life, science has little help to offer. We must all rely willy-nilly on mankind's ancient wisdom, traditionally expressed in the language of religion. There is a profound conflict between these two worldviews, but in practice, most scientists of my acquaintance have little trouble reconciling them.

Budding scientists commonly start out with adolescent fantasies about great discoveries, honors, prizes, and lasting fame. Few of us achieve those high ambitions, but we also learn that "success" is not what the life of a scholar and explorer is about. The rewards of science come chiefly from the doing, and I consider it an immense privilege to have spent my life pondering the wayward ways of nature rather than manufacturing widgets or chaffering in the marketplace. Like the clerics of old, who are our precursors in spirit, scientists are commonly a little removed from everyday affairs and all the better for that detachment.

I owe my conception of life and the universe to science, and my sense of what decency and honor demand to the wisdom traditions, especially to Judaism and Buddhism. But what I understand of how the real world works was largely shaped by the experience of growing up in the Middle East, by wide and eclectic reading, and by untiringly wandering the globe. Travel and a passion for history would seem to have little to do with science, but they all feed into a worldview that not infrequently steps outside the optimistic liberalism in which I was raised. It is sad but true that good intentions all too often pave the road to hell; that God has nailed the Devil into us, all of us; and that the Law of Unintended Consequences rules the roost. Freedom, Justice, and Law are great goods, but at the end of the day, the absolute need for order trumps them all. I still strive to see the world as it is, not as I wish it were, but quite often fall short. The great verities all turn out to be half-truths at best, and few things are quite what they are said to be. As the world twists and turns restlessly and ever faster, uncertainty is the order of the day, and the only sensible guiding principle is an open-minded skepticism.

On a Glass of Beer

When I was teaching at Colorado State University, my responsibilities included an outreach course for non-science majors called "Cells, Genes, and Molecules". Hoping to make contact with undergraduate minds, I would begin by explaining how science is like a glass of beer. It seldom worked – they quickly spotted that my natural tipple is wine – but the simile has some merit. The bulk of the beer is a clear golden liquid, nutritious and flavorful, but not much happens there except for some bubbles that rise to the top. In science, this would correspond to the huge volume of established systematic knowledge: the body of chemistry and physics, or what leaves and livers do. Questions and controversies do arise, within science and outside, and these bubbles reach the foaming head. The head is the realm of ideas, proposals, and speculations. Some are plausible notions, some long taken for granted, such as that species are immutable or that human affairs are ruled by the stars. Some are crazy notions, including wandering continents and that aliens from outer space left the vast ruins that dot the jungles of Central America. Between the foam and the beer is an interface, where bubbles are made and bubbles are broken. This is where science comes alive and where researchers make their home.

What is this pursuit called science? The word comes from *scientia*, Latin for knowledge, but refers to a particular province of knowledge. In the English-speaking world, "science" designates systematic organized knowledge about the natural world, excluding such subjects as history and theology (both of which could be called sciences in German). Furthermore, as a practical matter, we take science to be objective, public knowledge. My personal convictions, however certain they are to my mind, do not qualify as science and neither does secret proprietary knowledge restricted to some company. But "science" is a verb as well as a noun; it designates a special way of coming to know the world, of discovering true things about nature, and this is where the peculiar ways of the scientific community take center stage.

In principle we begin from the premise that we know nothing for certain; every belief, however widely held, is open to question, including the established truths of science itself. We look at the world around us and make guesses, more or less rational, about how things work and how they came about. Opinions are formally expressed as "hypotheses", tentative statements of what may be true, whose merits are then assessed by observation, reason, and whenever possible, by experiment. According to the Austrian philosopher Karl Popper, whose writings were enormously influential, a hypothesis is most fruitful when so formulated that it can be "falsified", i.e. shown to be wrong. Verification of my pet idea is nice and gratifying, but only shows that my hypothesis remains in the running. Disproof, by contrast, is powerful: Ideally, it closes off one line of thinking and forces me to look for another. A hypothesis that has withstood rigorous testing and that covers a broad range of observations will be described as a "theory"; think gravity or evolution. Unlike popular speech, which belittles "mere theory", among scientists that term is a high accolade, little short of certainty. To a remarkable degree, and unlike most other human pursuits, science admits (even celebrates) its mistakes and learns from them to do better. It is strange but true that the knowledge gained by insisting on perpetual uncertainty is as close as we can come to the truth about nature.

The chemiosmotic hypothesis of energy transduction by ion currents, which we touched upon in Chapters 4 and 5, makes an excellent example of scientific inquiry in the Popperian mode. Mitchell deliberately formulated it in such a way as to highlight assertions that were open to disproof. Is it true that membranes are generally impermeable to ions, including protons? Is it true that the respiratory chain, the photosynthetic apparatus, and the ATP synthase translocate protons from one side of the membrane to the other? Are the resulting gradients of the predicted polarity and magnitude, and are they required for cellular work such as nutrient uptake and ATP production? Most crucially, is it true that ATP synthesis by oxidative phosphorylation and photophosphorylation are absolutely dependent on closed, intact vesicular membranes? The fact that Mitchell's counter-intuitive proposals could be rigorously tested and confirmed by experiment is the chief reason why they ultimately overcame the disbelief of the community and are now respectfully referred to as the "chemiosmotic theory".

§

Science as we know it today, the rational and systematic pursuit of knowledge, is an invention of the West. Its roots go back to ancient Greece, and both the Arabs and the Chinese made numerous discoveries and useful inventions. But the contempo-rary way of doing science is a fruit of European civilization and part of the great turning from the medieval mind to the modern. The scientific revolution began in Astronomy, conventionally with Copernicus, and gathered steam in the 17th century. David Wootton, in his magisterial opus *The Invention of Science* places it between 1572, when Tycho Brahe first observed a new star in the sky, and the publication of Newton's treatise on optics in 1704. That century laid the foundations of an altogether fresh set of attitudes. It was a time when it became possible to think that the Ancients had not known all there was to know, that new truths could be (and had been) discovered, and that facts trump both tradition and authority.

Those who spoke the language of the new learning and lived by its precepts were never numerous (and are not all that common today), but they utterly transformed the way all of us perceive the world. As Wootton puts it, in 1600 a typical well-educated European would have believed in magic, witchcraft, and werewolves and that mice are born spontaneously in a pile of old rags. He held that base metals could be turned into gold and that comets portend evil. For him the earth stood still while the planets, sun, and stars circled around it, and he looked to Pliny, Galen, Ptolemy, and Plato for authoritative knowledge about nature and medicine. Little more than a century later, an educated Englishman (in the land where science first found public currency) lived in a different world. He had looked through a telescope, perhaps a microscope. No one of his class believed in witches, magic, alchemy, or astrology; he took it for granted that the earth travels around the sun and that creatures do not arise spontaneously. He was skeptical about miracles and might even harbor doubts about the literal veracity of the Bible. The world had been made afresh and would never again be perceived as it had been. From its original home in the northwest, science spread across Europe and beyond, concurrently with European power and example.

§

Among educated Westerners, it is largely taken for granted that science has indeed given us a better, more accurate understanding of the world than our predecessors had. Public confidence is bolstered by the overwhelming success of science-based technology and affirmed every time we board an airplane or ask the doctor for a prescription. Perversely, among philosophers and historians, a significant school of thought rejects the consensus;

proponents assert that science is a social construct, no different in principle from history or politics, and has no valid claim to objective truth. This view can be traced back to another important philosopher of twentieth-century science, Thomas Kuhn, and his influential thesis that (contrary to Popper) science grows by lurching from one conceptual framework to another. The crucial events in the history of science are scientific revolutions, episodes in which the conventional framework is overturned and replaced by another incompatible with the first. If so, is there any good reason why the new conventions should be any more permanent or true than those they displaced? Scientist generally agree that the advance of science often does entail a "paradigm shift" (Kuhn's term); as explained in earlier chapters, I was myself privileged to participate in a typical Kuhnian revolution. We also understand that scientific literature is not a compendium of certified verities, but the record of a continuing conversation about how best to make sense of reality. Still, very few scientists question that overall the arc of science bends toward a better, more truthful understanding of the world as it really is.

Science is progressive, of that I have no doubt. So are engineering and medicine, but the same cannot be said of most other endeavors (politics, anyone?). That does not mean that the advance of science is steady, uniform, or inevitable, nor that it necessarily leads to a world that is comprehensible to human minds or conducive to human happiness. Over the past 300 years, as knowledge exploded and demanded ever more technical terminology, the language of science has drifted ever farther from the common speech. A gulf has opened between "Us Who Speak Science" and take its viewpoint for granted and "Them" who often have little idea what we are up to and increasingly distrust our motives and good sense. Moreover, there may indeed be a real divergence of purpose: Science has largely succeeded in de-mystifying the world, but in so doing, it is stripping away much of the joy, magic, and meaning that people crave more than rational understanding. This may well be why the public seems to be turning away from science as a framework for learning, work, and a way of living.

Not in Kansas Anymore

It is quite startling to note how biological research has changed over the course of my lifetime. The profession I embraced as a young man was still a cottage industry, practiced in universities by a professor with a handful of students and postdocs. (The group in which I grew up, with 27 members, was uncommonly large and a harbinger of things to come.) Methods were simple and manual. I remember investing in an electronic pH-meter, as soon as they appeared on the market, to take the place of Hydrion Paper that changed color with the pH; that was a source of much frustration for me, for the critical range around neutrality coincided with my red-green color blindness. By the same token, a good binocular microscope represented a pinnacle of technical sophistication. Contrast this with a contemporary laboratory bench crowded with banks of complex and powerful instruments designed to tackle questions barely conceivable fifty years ago.

Today the computer is king over all, and his smack is felt in science as everywhere else. The kind of science that I practiced, which is still common in university departments, hangs on individual minds engaged in formulating and testing hypotheses. Ideas, evidence, and critical examination by experiment created our imposing edifice of objective public knowledge. The advent of computers has spawned a new and wholly different approach that dispenses with hypotheses. Instead, we celebrate the collection of vast sets of data, without any preconceived ideas about what we may find, which are then searched for unexpected relationships by powerful computational methods. The world is complicated, really complicated, and there are innumerable questions that can only be tackled with the aid of computers; in biology, think of phylogeny, protein folding, or the intricate signaling pathways that regulate the operation of cells. Correlations often do point the way to discovery, and as a physiologist I still hope that breakthroughs in understanding biological systems may be in the offing. But it remains to be seen whether hypothesis-free science can deliver real insights and change our perception of the world.

Concurrently with the transformation of methodology, the very goals of research have been re-directed. The small science of the 1950s through the 1970s successfully tackled many of the most fundamental issues in biology and drafted the outlines of our current understanding of life. By about 1980, the pillars that support the edifice were in place: the chemical structures of molecules and cells, metabolism and membranes, the nature and expression of genetic information, and how organisms harvest energy and harness it to the performance of work had all been worked out, at least in principle. I do not mean to disparage later advances, which include such mind-expanding discoveries as ribozymes, regulatory RNA, ancient DNA, and the triple-stemmed tree of life. But one cannot avoid the impression that by 1980 most of the low-hanging fruit had been picked, the conceptual framework was finished, and much of what has been done since fills in the gaps. Are there then no more mysteries to ponder? Sure there are, and we will touch on some in the second half of this book, but they call for a different mindset.

It is then not altogether surprising that the goals of research have shifted over time, from the quest for basic principles to their application in medicine, industry, agriculture, and warfare. But this internal transition coincided with, and was reinforced by, the drastic cultural transformation from the New Deal and the Great Society to the freewheeling market ideology that is dominant today. Erwin Chargaff, a distinguished chemist who made fundamental contributions to the elucidation of DNA structure, highlighted the trend in an article published in 1987. "[Society] was wont to rank science, until far into our century, among the highest and purest pursuits of mankind. Science was the never-ending search for truth about nature, a quest that would help us understand the workings of our world. That era has ended…a new era has begun: Science is now the craft of the manipulation, modification, substitution, and deflection of the forces of nature." Chargaff may have been a little gloomy – he habitually viewed the world through very dark glasses – but the truth of his vision seems to me undeniable.

Public funding of research in the United States and Western Europe is still generous, but costs have risen relentlessly (in part because of the reliance on ever more advanced technology), and there are now so many more hands stretched out for every dollar. Universities and other public institutions have ceased to grow, and some of the best are struggling to survive. Where once we raised money to support research, we now all too often promote research in order to raise funds. Few young scientists can look forward to a secure and productive career in academe; the great majority end up in industry, and all are increasingly buffeted by the harsh winds of economies in transition. No wonder the young, even more than the grey-haired, feel squeezed and pinched and wonder whether the rewards match the struggle.

The sheer volume of today's science has its own consequences, inconspicuous but large. Since professional advancement is linked to publication, the literature is growing explosively. According to a recent article, in the biomedical field alone, a million (sic) titles pour into the PubMed database every year. The result is a classic case of inflation: As the number of documents soars, the value of each one diminishes. The trend has been reinforced by the advent of open-access electronic journals, which charge authors a hefty fee but go lightly on critical review. It is becoming ever harder to keep up with the output even in one's own field, let alone with science in general, and for new ideas to get a proper hearing. In consequence, scientists are forced into ever more narrow specialization. What was traditionally called "scholarship" has not yet gone extinct, but is becoming uncommon.

The public, it seems, by and large still values science and trusts scientists to serve the public interest. But my strong sense is that people neither understand nor appreciate the search for knowledge for its own sake, which is what has historically motivated scientists. People crave the goodies that science brings, commonly in the form of technological products, and they fear the threats and perils that come along; basic science just does not resonate with the way most folks' minds work. Science has never been a profession for the masses and seems now to be becoming the aspiration of a shrinking minority. The era of spectacular progress in understanding seems to be passing; we shall not see it's like again.

Quo Vadis

Many of us, at one time or another, wrestle with the question "What is science good for?" Some argue that we do science because it is fun, and so it is, but that does not do justice to the enormous impact of science on all human affairs, especially over the past two centuries. Many more find the chief worth of science in the applications that touch people, as in medicine or agriculture; those are undeniable, but so are the baleful consequences, as in warfare and environmental degradation. It used to be fashionable to celebrate the role of science in subjugating nature, bending it to human will and purposes; we are not so sure today that this is always a cause for rejoicing. For myself, the true use of science is to make the world intelligible; an insight I drew from the writings of Loren Eiseley, naturalist and poet, during a personal crisis of doubt forty years ago. For several decades now that has been a guiding precept for me, gradually turning me from an experimentalist into a scholar and a generalist – one who knows a little about almost everything, but not a lot about anything.

I am old now, and that surely has something to do with my growing ambivalence about what we are doing. I believe that to make the world rationally intelligible is a scientist's chief duty and our great satisfaction as well. But knowledge has its dark side no less than the bright one. The continuing march of science has had tremendous consequences for all human activities; as our patterns of living have become increasingly based on our dominance over nature, economics and environment and medicine and warfare have all been transformed – for good and for ill. Even though I remain personally engaged in de-mystifying the world (see Part II), I badly miss the windy spaces of the unknown, the sheer wonder that once lent so much enchantment to the pursuit of rational understanding. And I can only dread the future that seems to be in store for our grandchildren: a dystopic, degraded, and de-humanized world ruled by overbearing intelligent machines. Judging by the short sci-fi stories that appear every week on the back page of *Nature*, many of them written by young scientists, I am not alone in my misgivings. Mankind has gained much, but we are also paying an enormous price for eating the fruit of the tree of knowledge. Science has unleashed a vast tide in the affairs of men, which is now sweeping us all along paths that no one has chosen, towards ends that no one can foresee.

The World on Fire

If one pays any attention at all to the news, it is hard to avoid a sense of bewilderment, dismay, and apprehension. What are we coming to, after all our vaunted progress in science and technology, not to mention the lessons of recent history? The domestic scene is disturbing enough, with the nation split down the middle on every issue and the political establishment gone dysfunctional, but we are still prosperous, at peace, and reasonably secure thanks to an ocean on each side. More alarming is the news from abroad, with the inexorable rise of an assertive

China, an increasingly bellicose Russia, Western Europe bogged down in bickering and swamped by a tide of refugees, Africa mired in poverty, and the Middle East sliding ever deeper into chaos. Is this just a stormy interlude in an otherwise progressive trend or portents of the impending collapse of civilization as we know it? The world is not about to come to an end, but we are clearly in the midst of drastic and wrenching changes that will leave the familiar political and economic landscape transformed in unpredictable ways. It would be preposterous to lay all the turmoil at the door of science, but insofar as science and science-based technology have done so much to shape the way we now think and live, science can hardly avoid all responsibility. What follows is a personal attempt to make some sense of what is going on, with the focus on trends rather than events.

Much of the continuing upheaval can be blamed on the deterioration of the order that has prevailed since the Second World War (and in some places the First). Domestically, we see the erosion of the social compact that traces back to the New Deal, when government took responsibility for the public welfare, the economy, and much else. Landmarks include social security, graduated income taxes, civil rights, environmental protection, and Federal support for science, education, and technology. This consensus has been losing ground ever since President Reagan came to power in 1980 and is being replaced by an ideology of free markets, business values, and individual liberty (especially economic, but also social). The signs include the pressure for ever-lower taxes, the decline of labor unions, and vociferous opposition to government supervision of the economy, education, and health care (even unto vaccinations). Perhaps one should include on this list the growing acceptability of drugs, alternative sexual lifestyles, and that peculiarly American obsession with guns! What all sides share is discontent and a sense that the nation is "on the wrong track", but there is no agreement on where the right track runs.

On the global level, the passing of the old order is generating much violence and anarchy. The postwar era was a golden age on the international stage, more peaceful (or at least less war-torn) than the century preceding World War II, and much of the credit should go to the restrained and benevolent hegemony exercised by the United States (assisted in no small measure by the universal terror inspired by nuclear weapons). American economic and military dominance established and enforced a global order based on liberal capitalism, open markets, democratic government, and religious liberty. To be sure, this Western pattern of order was never universally successful; it was strenuously opposed by the Soviet Union and some others, and more than once fell short of its ideals. But the United States presided over the dissolution of the colonial empires, kept at bay the tide of communism that threatened to swamp the world, avoided another global war, lifted millions out of poverty, and established a livable (if imperfect) society that most people found attractive and far preferable to the alternatives. This relatively benign period is clearly passing. I attribute some of the erosion to the inexorable decline of Western power, both economic and military, which now afflicts the United States as well as older empires. But much of the decline is relative to the ascent of nations that were once negligible, including China and Iran. As the West, and the United States in particular, turns inward and pulls in its horns, others step forward, often with rather more selfish motives. American fatigue with the world's never-ending troubles is understandable, but our children may pay the price for peace in our time.

§

Nowhere is the breakdown of the old order more glaring and more violent than in the Middle East, the Arab world in particular. Syria, Iraq, and Libya are disintegrating; Yemen looks to be on the same track. The destruction of lives, livelihoods, the whole traditional culture of the Arabs, overwhelms the imagination and has unleashed the largest exodus of refugees since the Second World War. Some islands of order are still hanging on – Jordan, Lebanon, Morocco – but the future seems to rest once again with hard-fisted authoritarian regimes (Egypt, the Gulf Emirates, Saudi Arabia; Iran is a relatively progressive member of that club). They justify their hold on power by their claim to maintain order and to restrain the tide of religious totalitarianism. Ever since the Iranian revolution of 1979 reignited the long-simmering frictions between Shia and Sunni, the fissures in the Islamic world have grown wider; and they now seem as unbridgeable as those that rent Europe during the wars of religion five centuries ago.

It is fashionable to blame the failure of the Arabs (indeed, of most Muslim nations) to establish societies that function effectively in the modern world on the authoritarian regimes that have ruled these lands in recent centuries: the Ottoman Turks, Ibn Sauds, Assads, Gaddafis. There is surely some truth in this argument, but I believe the problem goes much further back, into the roots of Islamic history. The fact is that the social and intellectual developments that made the West "western", underpin modernity, and fanned out across the globe, never happened in the Islamic sphere. Chief among them is secularism: religion still plays a major role in Western lives, but we regard it as a personal matter rather than the central organizing principle of society. The Islamic world has had no experiences that correspond to the Reformation, the Enlightenment, Rationalism, and the rise of science and democracy. Such ideas were present in embryo in the early Middle Ages, when the Muslim lands were the center of civilization, but they were stifled by the ascendancy of the clerics about a thousand years ago. In many ways, Muslims remain locked in a medieval mindset that revolves around God rather than Man. We may be watching an orgy of self-destruction not unlike that which convulsed Central Europe during the Thirty Years War, leaving a third of the population dead and turning vast swathes into wasteland. Can the Arabs pull themselves out of that death spiral? So far, at least, no one else has been willing or able to impose restraint; even if one did, the immediate result would be only to increase the carnage. We stand by and wring our hands in horror, but we may be unable to do more than to bind up the wounds of the survivors.

§

The events that dominate the headlines are like storm waves that sink ships and crash onto ocean shores. The winds and currents that drive the tempest are less conspicuous, but a little reflection turns up at least four long-term trends. In America, we give much weight to people's pent-up yearning for liberty, for a say in how their affairs are run, and that is surely real. It was popular rebellion that sparked the "Arab Spring" in 2011, that overthrew the Soviet Empire in 1989, drove the British out of India in 1947, and galvanized revolt all across Europe in 1848. And it is popular resentment that today animates the resistance of Tibetans to Chinese oppression and that of Palestinian Arabs to the Israeli occupation. But there are deeper currents that run beneath.

One is the relentless increase in the human population. In 1800, there were about one billion people on earth; by the time I was born, in 1929, the total was close to two billion, and it has swelled at an accelerating rate since. Between 1967 and the present, our numbers have doubled, and now stand at nearly seven billion. True, the rate of increase is slowing, but the total keeps rising. Optimists hope that the population will level out at around 9.5 billion and then begin a slow decline; pessimists project far larger numbers. The culprit is rising standards of nutrition and public health: It does not cost much to provide clean water, dispose of sewage, and vaccinate children. So the children live, grow up, and propagate in their turn. Most of the projected increase will occur in the world's poorest nations, especially in Africa and southern Asia. By any human standard, all this represents progress, but it has inescapable consequences. There is no longer much unused arable land on earth, and the pressure on water resources are plain to see in many places (the Middle East, for one). We are in the midst of a global mass extinction of wildlife, driven in large part by loss of habitat. Is it any surprise that people seek to escape the desperate circumstances in their homeland, be they outright war or merely economic hopelessness? How many more people can the earth sustain and at what cost?

The second long-range trend is the deterioration of the global environment. Its nature and extent vary from place to place, but it afflicts most of the globe: the visible pollution of air and water in China and India, deforestation all across the tropics, ocean fisheries depleted despite efforts to rein in harvesting, cities swelling beyond their capacity to provide basic services. Still more ominous, the signals of global climate change are becoming unmistakable, particularly in northern latitudes. I can find some sympathy for politicians who avoid facing up to the trend. After all, this is a global threat, not a local or national one, so that what we do here in the United States will have only a limited impact. The magnitude of the problem is enormous, solutions will reach deep into every aspect of economic, political, and personal life, and no one really knows how to tackle it. Still, it almost defies belief that some politicians who aspire to national leadership continue to deny that the problem even exists.

The third great current is what I think of as "technological drive", the continuous pressure to build more powerful and faster machines to do our bidding. The changes wrought thereby have been apparent ever since the industrial revolution and are now reaching into every aspect of the economy, education, medicine, and warfare. What the railroads did to coach travel, television did to entertainment and politics; and where the Internet is now taking us is anyone's guess. Computers fuel globalization as well as ballistic missiles; they have opened the way into space, and also made it possible to wreak havoc across vast distances. The world is awash in weaponry, more powerful than ever before and beyond anyone's capacity to suppress. Will artificial intelligence be the next frontier in our capacity for destruction? No one is in charge; no one is in control. We are bouncing along like balls in a mountain stream towards ends that no one can foresee.

Many years ago, the British novelist Mary Renault wrote a story called "The Last of the Wine". It chronicles the lives of several families in ancient Athens, just before the outbreak of the Peloponnesian War; cultured and intelligent folks, they go about their affairs utterly unaware that their world is about to be swept away forever. The title has haunted me for years, for I suspect that this is what we, too, are doing: sipping (nay, gulping) the last of the wine. We thought that we had outgrown wars of religion, wanton destruction, and unbridled savagery, but we are far from it, as the news reminds us every day, and the long-range trends do not bode well. More than ever, the world seems like a seething cauldron, with civilization a crust that keeps our worst impulses from reaching the surface. Thicker in some places than in others, the crust everywhere requires constant upkeep and frequent repair, often with the use of force. When the crust of order fractures, all hell breaks loose.

Americans are optimists by nature and inclined to dismiss such forebodings as expressions of the melancholia that is bred in the bones of many Central Europeans. It may be so, or perhaps not.

PART II: THE PERPLEXING PHENOMENON OF LIFE

Introduction

Biology, my dictionary tells me, is the study of living organisms – how they are built, how they work, and how they came to be that way. The enterprise has been spectacularly successful, generating a huge body of solid knowledge concerning all the levels of biology from molecular genetics to the operations of entire ecosystems. Strangely, the one question that is seldom broached nowadays is the one that defines our subject: What is life, how does it relate to the inanimate world of physics and chemistry, and how did it arise from the dust of the cosmos when the earth was young?

As our knowledge has grown beyond the grasp of any single one of us, we have gained some appreciation of just how strange living things are. Intricate and complex, they obey all the laws of physics and chemistry, yet their existence could never have been predicted from those laws. Life stands squarely within the material world, but at the same time seems to stand apart, flaunting its autonomy, purposeful behavior, and in one instance, the capacity to reflect on its own nature. Now that we know most of what is worth knowing about the way living things work, we need to integrate all this mass of facts into a comprehensible framework: in a phrase, to make biology intelligible. The question "What is Life?" is not one for the laboratory scientist; you can't get a grant to study that. But it is a proper subject for a natural philosopher, and over the past two decades, I have become obsessed with it.

The object of the chapters that follow is to summarize my understanding of life as a phenomenon of nature, in a manner comprehensible to readers who have little knowledge of science but appreciate its aims. Albert Einstein once wrote that everything should be made as simple as possible, but not simpler; and I have tried to heed his advice. So the present account blithely ignores the ifs, buts, and exceptions that bedevil every general statement about living things; it omits all technicalities and details; and it shamelessly oversimplifies for the sake of clarity. I have also omitted the references to the work of others that scholarly etiquette demands, while drawing freely on their findings and writings. But the problem remains that life is inherently complicated, not because overspecialized scientists make it so but because complexity is built into its very fabric.

All the same, the upshot of the inquiry is clear enough. We understand quite well "what life is", and we know most of the essentials about how it works. We know rather less about how the living world came to be as we find it and very little about its ultimate origin. This state of affairs is at once frustrating and exhilarating. We scientists like to believe that it is our task to demystify the world, to make it rationally intelligible; and it turns out that the world is by no means inscrutable and yields quite readily to our prodding and probing – up to a point. Only when we ask the very deep questions (What came before the Big Bang? How does mind emerge from matter? How did life begin?), do we seem to run into serious barriers. It remains to be seen whether reason and technology can overcome all obstacles, or whether there are real limits to what we can know.

8: Strange Objects

One of the fundamental characteristics common to all living beings without exception [is] that of being objects endowed with a purpose or project, which...they exhibit in their structure and carry out through their performances.

—Jaques Monod, *Chance and Necessity*

A Singular State of Matter

Let me begin by stating the obvious: The objects we see all around us fall neatly into two classes – those that are alive and those that are not. Mountains, rocks, clouds, and rivers are "inanimate". Their forms, transformation over time, and eventual fate are determined entirely by forces from outside the objects themselves. The hulking bulk of Mount Rainier is often said to brood over my hometown of Seattle, benevolent in some moods and menacing in others; Native Americans consider it a god. But we know now that Mount Rainier was sculpted by volcanic ructions, by snow and water, and these – rather than any volition of its own – will shape its future. Animals, plants, even microbes are different, quite strikingly so. Living things drive and guide their own activities, whose ultimate purpose is persistence, survival, and reproduction. Their forms are produced by forces of their own making and are quite faithfully passed from one generation to the next with the aid of an internal program. Inanimate objects are made; living things make themselves.

At the same time, living things are part of the same world of physics and chemistry that rules the clouds and threw up Mount Rainier. That became abundantly clear when, beginning in the 19th century, living things were subjected to chemical dissection. It turned out that living things are made of lifeless molecules. Their chief elements are carbon, hydrogen, nitrogen, oxygen, phosphorus, and sulfur (CHNOPS), with many other elements present in trace amounts. Every organism is composed of millions, even billions of molecules, of many hundreds of different kinds. Most of these molecules are found in nature only in the context of living things. Yet the laws that govern the structures and interactions of biological molecules are no different from those that produce inorganic minerals, and most biological molecules can nowadays be synthesized in the laboratory. No "vital force" unique to life has ever been found. So life is chemistry, but chemistry of a very special sort. To borrow an evocative phrase from Stuart Kauffman, it seems that life has explored realms of physics and chemistry that inanimate objects never enter. The more I reflect on this, the more impressed I am by the division of the material world into two classes – things that live and things that don't.

As a rule, nature dislikes sharp categories; she prefers her boundaries fuzzy. But in the case of life, there are very few ambiguous cases, and most of those vanish upon closer inspection. True, one candle lights another, but not by repro-duction; the size and shape of each flame is determined by its own wax, not by the donor of the light. Crystals grow them-selves and supply seeds for another crop of crystals, but again heredity is not involved. Machines make a subtler instance: intricate and purposeful, machines share many features with living organisms, but even the most sophisticated robot cannot make itself. That day may come, and then we shall have to think afresh, but for the present, all machines are artifacts of life, accessories to the biological universe but not themselves alive. Freeze-dried bacteria are another intriguing case because many of them recover when placed in a nutritious medium. They were alive once and may be alive in the future, but they are not alive now. Still, freeze-dried bacteria underscore a crucial principle to which we shall return: the importance of structure. The only objects that do straddle the line between life and non-life are viruses. Simple viruses are "mere" chemicals. They form crystals, and some can be made by chemists in the laboratory, yet they grow, multiply, and evolve all too quickly. Besides, their chemical makeup (proteins, nucleic acids, sometimes lipids) assures us that viruses belong to the universe of living things.

Most readers will probably agree that living and non-living designate distinct classes of objects, but some will not. Spiritually inclined persons sometimes hold that rivers and mountains also have souls, that everything is alive, and that spirit or mind, rather than matter, is the essence of the universe. I shall not argue the point, which stems from an altogether dif-ferent usage of the concept of "living". Whatever merit there may be in the spiritual take on the world, it seems to miss one of its most remarkable features: that it holds an abundance of those strange material objects that possess "life".

We Know Life When We See It

Life and living are fiendishly difficult to define, but easy enough to recognize. Life is a quality or attribute of objects that draw matter and energy from their surroundings, build and maintain themselves, and reproduce their own kind. It is a natural phenomenon, just like tides, earthquakes, and the change of the seasons. Just how living things are constructed and how they work is the stuff of modern science, whose range and volume vastly exceed what I can touch on here. Let me instead focus on a few aspects that bear directly on the nature of life and that should be part of the mental furniture of anyone who aspires to a measure of scientific literacy.

Perhaps the first thing you notice when you begin to explore the universe of living things is its staggering diversity. There are cabbages and there are kings, both living but grossly different. We have towering redwoods, the tiny spiders that live in the crevices of their bark, bacteria and protozoa in the guts of those spiders, and mushrooms all 'round. What do these have in common, apart from being alive? At first sight, nothing at all, but that turns out to be fallacious. When we examine not the forms and workings of the organisms but their chemical makeup, we find a surprising degree of uniformity. All of them are made up of substances of the same kind, such as proteins, nucleic acids, lipids, and a collection of small "metabolites", substances that occur in nature only in the context of living things. This is not to say that all organisms are chemically the same, far from it;

but it clearly indicates that all living things are related, members of a huge extended family. We might have guessed that from the obvious fact that we all eat one another (as Darwin did), but the unity of biochemistry underscores a fundamental truth: All life on earth is of one singular kind.

A second, subtler general feature of living things is "organized complexity", visible at every level from chemistry and structure to whole ecosystems. The common term "organisms", in use since the 18ᵗʰ century, implies both organization and complexity. Scholars continue to bicker over just what is meant by complexity, but it is clearly a function of the number of parts and the ways they interact. An airplane is visibly more complex than a bicycle, which in turn surpasses a wheelbarrow. The number of molecules that go to make up even the simplest organism boggles the mind. A typical individual bacterium is likely to be a short cylinder, not unlike a propane tank in shape, but only 2 to 3 micrometers long and 1 micrometer in diameter. Far too small to see with the naked eye, we would have to line up 500 of them end to end to reach the thickness of a dime; it would take a thousand billion to fill a thimble. But this minute speck of life holds some 2 to 3 million protein molecules of several hundred sorts; 20 million molecules of fatty lipids; and some 300 million small molecules and ions. Let's not forget water, the most abundant constituent, with some 40 billion molecules. All this in just one tiny cell; an amoeba, a thousand times larger by volume than the bacterium, holds correspondingly more molecules.

Complexity of composition is common in nature; a pinch of mud probably rivals a cell in complexity. But the complexity of a cell is different; it has purpose, and that is what the word "organization" conveys. These are very particular molecules, most of which serve a purpose or "function" in the operation of the organism. Many are components of minuscule machines that zip together amino acids to make proteins, transport cargo around the cell, or rotate like a propeller to make it move. Almost all the molecules are arranged in space in a particular pattern that is reproduced in every organism of a given kind. It clearly takes an awful lot of parts, each one in its proper location, to make the whole – the collective – work as it should inorder to persist and reproduce. It is this organized complexity, its nature and origin, that have come to fascinate me.

The first manifestation of organized complexity was recognized in the mid-nineteenth century: All organisms, large and small, are constructed from basic units that came to be called "cells". Many – in fact, the great majority – are "unicellular"; they consist of a single cell. A minority, which includes all the creatures large enough to see with the unaided eye (animals, plants, fungi), are "multicellular", aggregates of numerous cells – millions or billions of them. The human brain alone consists of some 80 billion cells! Each cell is itself a unit of life that makes and reproduces itself. It is invariably enclosed in a surface structure made up of one or several membranes that keep the cell's interior (its "cytoplasm") separate from the world outside and distinctive in composition and activities. And here is another remarkable feature that should be shouted from the rooftops: Cells arise only by reproduction, every cell from a previous cell, and never ever appear *de novo* out of non-living matter. Truly, as W.S. Beck said many years ago, "The cell is the microcosm of life for in its origin, nature, and continuity reside the entire problem of biology."

As microscopes grew sharper and more powerful, they revealed ever more structure and organization. Initially the term "cell" signified little more than a blob of cytoplasm bounded by a surface (the "plasma membrane"), with a central dot called the kernel, or "nucleus". By now we recognize two kinds of cellular organization: the small and relatively simple cells of "prokaryotes", the Bacteria and Archaea, whose true complexity only becomes apparent at the molecular level; and the larger and visibly intricate cells of "eukaryotes", the cells that make up animals, plants, fungi, and protozoa. They are endowed with a discrete nucleus; visible chromosomes; a suite of organelles including mitochondria; sometimes chloroplasts; a conspicuous network of internal membranes and compartments; and a cytoskeleton. Of the myriads of molecules that make up cells, only some are free to slosh around ("diffuse") in the cytoplasm. Most have a fixed abode in one intracellular structure or another, and their functions demand that they be in their proper place.

Order at all levels – molecular, structural, and functional – is a crucial aspect of life and the key to the entire phenomenon. Regularity and predictability are not uncommon in nature (think crystals or the solar system), but organization (purposeful order) is rare. Living things are the only known example, and their degree of order vastly exceeds that of anything else. As Rupert Riedl (1925-2005), a Viennese zoologist who pioneered the systematic study of biological order, put it with pardonable hyperbole: "Life is order, pure and simple."

Life is short, we say, at least shorter than we wish. But the history of life is very long, almost as long as that of the earth itself. Geologists tell us that the earth was formed by the accretion of cosmic dust about 4.6 billion years ago. We do not know when life first appeared, but by 3.5 billion years ago, some rocks show indications of having originated in biological processes, and there are even some fossils that almost certainly represent cells. They look exactly like contemporary prokaryotes, the Bacteria and Archaea, and presumably lived in much the same way. The larger and structurally more elaborate eukaryotic cells (more precisely, fossils generally interpreted as the remains of eukaryotic cells) also go well back in time, but not nearly as far as prokaryotes do: The most ancient of those fossils date to about 1.6 billion years ago. Since eukaryotes, and they alone, gave rise to all the "higher faculties", those somewhat ambiguous fossils mark a milestone second in importance only to the origin of life itself. Multicellular organisms make their first appearance later still, a mere 600 million years ago.

This thumbnail sketch of life's history supplies an essential framework for inquiry into the origins of organization. First of all, it is a history, not a sudden creation. Taking the findings at face value, it appears that life began with small and relatively simple cells of the prokaryotic grade; it took two billion years to attain the complexity of eukaryotic cells, and another billion to grow large enough to be seen with the naked eye. For about three quarters of life's history, all the life that lived consisted of microorganisms, and they still make up the great majority of organisms in our day. Clearly, all the basic characteristics of life were established at the unicellular level, billions of years ago. Muscles, livers, leaves, embryos, cancer, and immune defense mechanisms all came much later, mind and consciousness later still. If you seek to understand the nature of life, your proper study is not mankind but cells, specifically microbial cells. This is why this inquiry centers on organisms seemingly remote from human concerns, especially bacteria, and has nothing to say regarding humans and higher creatures even though it is these that dominate most of our waking hours. By the time higher organisms appeared on earth, late in the game, the phenomenon of life was deeply rooted and fixed in outline.

9: Cells, Genes, and Molecules

Much of contemporary cell biology is but high-level botanizing... The central problem of biology is not so much the gathering of information as the comprehension of it.
—John Maddox, *What Remains to be Discovered*, 1998

Putting Energy to Work

In the inanimate world, events follow a predictable course. Water flows downhill, hot bodies cool, paint peels off the wall, things fall apart. Living things are different: They actively seek food, keep themselves warm, maintain their structure in the face of decay; they grow, multiply, and evolve over time generating mounting levels of organization. This in no way contradicts the laws of physics, because living things capture energy from a source in their environment and harness it to the performance of work. They are not entirely unique in this regard: Every washing machine or automobile does the same. Note, though, that machines are man-made objects, and to that extent, themselves part of the biological world. Machines are not alive, and organisms are not machines. But they share important and instructive features, and the metaphor of the machine pervades biology.

There is no mystery about what "energy" and "work" mean in everyday life, but now we need to be a little more rigorous. Work is the easier to grasp. Climbing stairs is a familiar example, physical work, and physicists measure that work by the force required and the distance over which it acts. Pumping up a bicycle tire is work and so is the accumulation of any substance (e.g., potassium ions) by living cells. But synthesizing a large and complex molecule with a specified structure, such as a protein, is also a kind of work. Broadly speaking, doing anything that goes counter to the spontaneous tendency of natural events is work. So air leaking out of the tire, the spontaneous tendency, requires no work; pumping it in takes work and can only be accomplished with an input of "energy". Most of what organisms do qualifies as work.

So what is energy? Its actual nature is elusive and would take us too far afield. Let us be content with defining it as the capacity to do work, a quality possessed by matter whenever it is in an unstable state, far from equilibrium. A can full of gasoline is in principle unstable; a match can set it alight, releasing lots of energy in the form of heat and light – but it can also be harnessed to make my car run up the hill and do work. That is what living things do: They harness natural sources of energy to do the kinds of work they find useful, including movement, transport, biosynthesis, and maintenance.

The world is full of processes that can potentially serve as sources of energy – a burning log, the sun's heat, lightning, wind, the tides and so on – but living things rely almost exclusively on two of them: light and the breakdown of preformed organic substances by chemical reaction with atmospheric oxygen. (This bland assertion omits those organisms that live by geochemical reactions, which will become prominent in Chapter 10). The phrase to conjure with is "energy coupling": How do living things capture the energy inherent in the oxidation of, say, a lump of sugar (or in a beam of light) and harness it to the performance of work? We all know that an automobile engine carries out a controlled combustion of gasoline, channeled by the design of the engine and its accessories so as to make the wheels go 'round. What is the equivalent process in living cells? This is the "coupling problem", and by the middle of the 20th century, it had become the burning issue in biochemistry. Its resolution by Peter Mitchell in the 'sixties made a revolution in bioenergetics and forged a quite unexpected link between the harvesting of energy and the organized structure of living matter. For me personally, the years of engagement with Mitchell and bioenergetics shaped all subsequent reflections on life, the universe, and all that.

To recapitulate briefly what was said in earlier chapters, living organisms harvest energy in electrical form. What happens is not unlike what goes on in a coal-fired power plant, where energy from burning coal is converted into a current of electrons; electricity is portable and can be connected to many appliances. Likewise, organisms process foodstuff chemically and ultimately feed the products into a device (the respiratory chain) that "burns" them and captures the energy released in the form of a current of charged particles. However, in organisms the current is carried by particles that bear a positive charge, most commonly protons (hydrogen ions). Light energy is harvested in a similar manner: Light is absorbed by specialized pigments including chlorophyll and eventually converted into a current of protons (Fig. 4.1).

The connection to cell structure stems from the fact that energy capture and transformation take place at the lipid membranes that bound all cells and organelles. The respiratory chain (and also the apparatus of light absorption) is built into and across a membrane in such a way that, when sugar is oxidized, protons are pumped from one side to the other. Lipid membranes naturally form closed vesicles and are largely impermeable to protons and other substances, except by way of specific portals. Proton extrusion generates an electrical potential across the membrane, which pulls the protons back whence they came. But they can only respond by flowing through devices cleverly constructed so as to allow that flux while harnessing the energy to some useful purpose. Some cell functions are driven directly by the proton current, but the most important of the devices that harness the current is the ATP synthase, an intricate enzymatic machine that uses the energy to generate ATP; this, in turn, supports most cellular operations.

It is a complicated and quite counter-intuitive way to harvest energy, but it has the virtue of great flexibility: Any energy source that can be made to drive a proton pump becomes available for biological work. Energy capture by way of ion currents has proven to be one of the universals of biology. All cells, apparently without exception, make use of an ion current to couple energy to work (albeit with numerous variations upon this general theme). To the best of my knowledge, no cell lacks the ATP synthase and some of its accessories. This discovery is quite certainly rich in meaning. Ubiquitous processes are probably very ancient, invented early, and retained ever since. The universality of ion currents suggests that membranes and chemical reactions organized across them were part and parcel of cellular life from the start. In the Beginning was the Membrane!

A Blueprint for a Cell?

Order (as in regularity and predictability) is common enough in nature; organization (purposeful order) is very rare. Living things are the prime example, but there is a second class of familiar objects that display organization, namely our own machines. Like living organisms, machines are made up of multiple parts that have particular functions and interact with other parts; they draw energy into themselves, sometimes matter also, and they are obviously purposeful. Machines cannot make, maintain, or reproduce themselves; they are not alive. But machines do share important features with living organisms, and since we know how to build them, we understand what they are. Ever since the 17th century, machine metaphors have pervaded the language of biology.

Machines are constructed for a purpose, in accordance with a plan or design. Is there a comparable blueprint for organisms? Not exactly, but genes serve an analogous function. The way organisms store, express, and transmit information from one generation to the next has features in common with a special class of machines, namely computers, and so students of heredity and evolution speak routinely of tapes that are read, translated, spliced, and corrected.

The discovery of how heredity works is one of the outstanding achievements of twentieth-century biology. By now the subject is taught in school, and most readers will be generally familiar with the essentials; let a brief and simplified recapitulation suffice here. Most of what cells do is done by proteins; they make up the enzymes, transport carriers, scaffolding and structures that constitute the machinery of life. Proteins are linear molecules, composed of amino acids strung together head to tail in chains 300 to 1000 units long. All proteins are constructed from a standard set of 20 amino acids, which are among the universals of biology, but the number of amino acids and their order (their sequence) varies from one protein to another. Transmission of a trait or character (e.g., the ability to use lactose) from parent to offspring requires getting the latter to make proteins of the correct sequence. The proteins themselves are not usually passed to the next generation; rather it is the capacity to make those proteins.

The instructions for making proteins are stored in another linear molecule, this one a nucleic acid called deoxyribonucleic acid, or DNA, which is the genetic material of all living cells. DNA consists of two complementary nucleic acid chains wound around each other to make a double helix. When cells reproduce, DNA is duplicated precisely; one copy remains with the mother cell, the other goes to the daughter. The information that specifies the amino acid sequences of proteins is stored in DNA in the form of sequences of nucleotides, again like letters in a word. To a very first approximation, it helps to conceive of a gene as the length of DNA that specifies one particular protein, which in turn corresponds to one simple trait (such as the ability to use lactose).

In itself, DNA does nothing; it is only a repository of sequence information, which becomes useful when it is "expressed". The DNA sequence (e.g. ABDC) is first "transcribed" into a more portable sequence, another nucleic acid called RNA (e.g. abdc). This is then "translated" into a different language, the sequence of amino acids in a protein. Each amino acid is specified by a particular triplet of nucleotides; the table of correspondences is known as the genetic code, which is the same for all organisms on earth. Translation is a complicated operation carried out by specialized molecular machines called ribosomes. These, again, are in principle universal: All cells make proteins with the aid of ribosomes, which operate by a universal mechanism but differ in detail among the major kinds of cells. As newly made proteins emerge, they fold spontaneously into the configuration required for their function in the cellular economy. We shall return to ribosomes many times below.

DNA replication, transcription, and translation are all highly accurate, but occasional mistakes do happen. An error in DNA sequence, a "mutation", is likely to be transmitted to the next generation. It may cause a change in the amino acid sequence of the protein, which that gene specifies, and quite possibly alter or abolish its function. Mutations are an important source of biological variation, and therefore serve as one of the raw materials of evolution.

The discovery of the structure of DNA, and of the mechanisms responsible for the expression and replication of genetic information, made an enormous impression on all who think about life. Today we march under a banner that depicts the double helix and proclaims that "DNA makes RNA makes protein". The factual findings were soon generalized into a far broader doctrine: All of heredity depends on DNA, which specifies all the traits and activities of living things. DNA has come to be seen as the master molecule, the secret of life itself. Francois Jacob, one of the giants of the heroic phase of molecular biology, famously wrote that "the whole plan of growth, the whole series of operations to be carried out, the order and the site of synthesis and their coordination, are all written out in the genetic message." Scientists as well as the public agree with Renato Dulbecco that: "Life is the execution of the instructions spelled in the genes." Twenty years later, the human genome was touted as the very blueprint of human life. And there is truth in this, important truth. Genetic information, its transcription and translation, are indeed central to heredity and to the way life works. The question is not whether it is important, but whether it is sufficient, and that turns out to be a rather more subtle question.

The Emergent Cell

Anyone who has watched a dividing cell doing it (or merely tried to follow the plot in a biology textbook) will have been impressed by the complexity of the choreography. Imagine reproducing an airliner the way cells divide, and you get an inkling. Duplicating the molecules, millions of them of thousands of different kinds, is the easy part. Cells must also reproduce the pattern, the arrangement of those molecules in space – everything from ribosomes and membranes to nuclei, organelles, and the genomic instructions too. All the while, the cell as a whole remains intact and functional. Even bacteria, so small and featureless when examined under a microscope, turn out to have quite an elaborate spatial organization, including a nucleoid and a cytoskeleton. How much of this organization and its reproduction are spelled out by genes? Does the genome specify cellular architecture, and if so, how are the instructions carried from a linear sequence on the scale of nanometers to a three-dimensional body at least a thousand-fold larger? As usual, bacteria as the simplest of cells make a good vehicle for reflection.

A set of remarkable experiments from the laboratory of J. Craig Venter throws the issue into sharp relief. Very briefly, what Venter's team has done is to replace the genome of one bacterial species by that of another species, and to document that cells that issue from the transplantation belong to the species that donated the DNA. Working with *Mycoplasma*, which has a particularly small genome and other virtues, they isolated the complete genome from one species (here designated D, for Donor) in the form of pure, naked DNA; transferred it into the cells of a second species (R, for Recipient); and then removed the original genome of the Recipient cells. Most cells of either the D or the R species are killed off during the procedure, and only the very few survive in which the genome from D was successfully transplanted into R cells. These (about 1 in some 150,000) grow into normal cells that are unambiguously of the Donor species. By the time the transplants have multiplied into a colony, about a million fold, no evidence of residual R genes or gene products could be detected. In other words, cell form and functions are ultimately determined by what the DNA prescribes, without any contribution from the cytoplasm or cell structure. In subsequent work, the team synthesized the entire genome chemically (a major feat in itself) and transplanted it into R cells, which were then enucleated. Again, the cells that grew out were of the D species. Most recently, the team used these procedures to create a "synthetic" cell with a genome somewhat smaller than that of any natural *Mycoplasma*: a mere 473 genes, which is presently the best approximation to the smallest gene set that can sustain cellular life. Even so, the function of a third of these genes is unknown.

Can we then safely conclude that all the instructions required to build a cell are encoded in its genome? No, because read-out of the genome evidently requires a functional cell at all times. Part of the reason is obvious. DNA by itself is inert, so readout requires a cell's household functions: enclosure, energy, building blocks, the apparatus of gene expression, and so on. The interesting question is whether the cytoplasm, or cell structure, are needed because they also make a more subtle contribution. The answer, it now appears, is yes.

The most important contribution to cell propagation that comes from outside the genome is membranes; in the genome transplantation experiments, that would be the plasma membrane. There have been numerous observations, going back decades, to indicate that membranes are never made afresh; they grow by extension of a previous membrane. The molecular mechanisms that insert proteins into membranes with the correct orientation also ensure that every membrane is architecturally continuous with its parent. To be sure, those proteins themselves are specified by genes, and the lipid matrix is produced by genetically specified enzymes. But the organization of these elements into a working membrane is carried over from the previous generation by virtue of their structural continuity. (Let me add that the assertion that spatial organization is transmitted by structural heredity rests, not on proof positive, but on the absence of any known exceptions. I hope that the program on which Venter's team has embarked will supply an experimental test of this claim.)

We have already encountered a specific example of the critical importance of membrane architecture when we spoke of energy transduction by a proton current (Chapters 4, 5, and above). All the chemical reactions are effected by proteins and specified by genes. But there is no gene for oxidative phosphorylation: that is a function of the system as a whole. It depends, not only on having the correct proteins but also on having them all together in a single closed vesicle, and with the correct orientation. It is an "emergent" property, manifested by the collective but not discernable in any of its components.

The grand example of an emergent property that depends on the proper organization of gene-specified elements is morphogenesis, the production of cell form. In recent years, our knowledge of how the shapes of bacteria come about (spheres, rods, spirals, and others) has grown explosively; and while much remains to be learned, we now appreciate the sophistication of the performance. Bacterial cells do not transcribe and translate genes and then wait for the products to fall into place. They grow, building the new cell upon its parent, so that the new is architecturally continuous with the old. This entails enlargement of the pattern of organization, locating a division site, and constructing the requisite apparatus just there; all the while, the cell retains its integrity and functional arrangements. Some of the instructions for doing this are in the genes, not explicitly but by implication. Ribosomes, for example, are produced by self-assembly of the proteins and nucleic acids, which together make up that clever machine; self-assembly is not spelled out in the genes that specify the proteins, yet the process requires the molecular parts to have the correct form for self-assembly. The capacity for self-organization, with or without an input of energy, is a major element in cell morphogenesis. Others include spatial markers and mechanical forces applied in the right place and in the right direction by means of an oriented cytoskeleton. No, it's not simple, and it's not all in the genes; the more we learn, the more we realize that the engineering metaphors of blueprints and programs are fundamentally misleading.

We don't have all the answers, but one can begin to make out the principles by which cells grow, shape themselves, and put in place their characteristic organization. Cells fall into the category of "systems", objects composed of multiple interacting elements forming a collective identity. More specifically, they are *dynamic* systems that draw matter and energy into themselves, maintain their collective identity despite the continuous turnover of their molecular parts, and reproduce their own kind with high fidelity. In the universe of systems, living things are in a class by themselves, and extreme order is the key to their persistence. Organisms persist, not because of any inherent stability, but by relentlessly reproducing their mode of organization. This requires operations at two levels: the genetic and the physiological. The genome does not, as commonly believed, direct all cellular operations. Genes are the indispensable repository of the information that specifies molecular structures and must be accurately transmitted from parents to offspring. But a growing and dividing cell must also recreate the pattern of organization that brings molecules to life, and this is not spelled out in the genes. Instead, it is inherited by virtue of the structural continuity that links every cell generation to its parents and to its offspring. Membranes, landmarks of spatial architecture, and probably other features are transmitted in this manner. If there is a blueprint for cellular organization, it is not DNA alone, but the cellular system as a whole. For more than 3 billion years, through thick and thin and with many changes over time, the successful transmission of cell organization has allowed life to flourish, multiply, and inherit the earth.

On the face of it, there seems to be a glaring conflict between the geneticist's understanding of cell organization and the physiologist's. The former insists that form and organization obey the genome's writ. The latter sees the genome as a key subroutine within the larger program of the cell, and it is the cell rather than its genome that grows, reproduces, and organizes itself. They can't both be true – or can they? We are coming to realize that these two points of view are complementary, not opposites. Heredity and reproduction operate on different timescales. A growing cell relies on self-organization to transmit much of its spatial order, by mechanisms that are often independent of the genetic instructions. But the genes specify the parts, the parts instruct the whole, and on the evolutionary timescale, it will be the genes that chiefly shape cells. Having said that, there remains a long stretch between the straightforward determination of the order of amino acids in a protein by its corresponding sequence of nucleotides and the devious and cryptic manner in which the genome can be said to specify the whole cell. Intellectual sloppiness must not obscure the conceptual shift from a linear chain of command to a branched and braided loop of causes and effects reverberating in a self-organizing web. The only agent capable of interpreting the genome of the bacterium *E. coli* as "a short rod with hemispherical caps" is the cell itself; and that is why it still takes a cell to make a cell. If you detect a whiff of vitalism about this, even a hint of heresy, then so let it be.

10: The Tapestry That Weaves Itself

A theory is the more impressive the greater the simplicity of its premises, the more different kinds of things it relates, and the more extended its area of applicability.
—Albert Einstein

Darwin's Truth

Like other Big Words, "Life" has more meanings than one. Thus far I have used it to designate the signature quality of molecular systems of daunting complexity that draw matter and energy into themselves, maintain their identity, reproduce their own kind, and evolve over time. But "life" also serves as shorthand for the totality of all such systems that make up so much of our daily experience: the plants, animals (including humans), even microbes. It also covers similar objects that lived in the past and are known to us only as fossils – mammoths, dinosaurs, ammonites, and bacteria of billions of years ago. Life in this collective sense offers a perspective complementary to that focused on organisms, like the difference between a forest and the trees. It is true today, and has probably been true from the beginning, that organisms never occur singly or in aggregates of a single kind. They invariably appear as members of a community or ecosystem whose citizens differ in size, form, and lifestyle, but whose habits and lives are intertwined. How did the multiplicity and variety of living forms come to be?

There are ultimately only two ways to account for the existence of life. One postulates an act of creation on the part of one or more gods, so that life reflects the mind and will of its creator(s). This belief has satisfied generations of people, and millions continue to find meaning in it today. It has inspired theologians, philosophers, painters, and poets, and it lies at the root of all Western societies. Only a minority embraces the alternative view, that the living world owes nothing to divine intervention but is wholly the product of natural causes acting over billions of years. The theory of evolution, articulated by Charles Darwin in 1859 in a book entitled *The Origin of Species*, shook up European society in its day and continues to reverberate in our time.

The principles are simple, but their potential consequences are almost unlimited. The traits and characteristics of organisms are passed on to their offspring with high fidelity, but not perfectly. Accidents do happen, mistakes occasionally occur during reproduction; some of these can be passed on to the next generation to be inherited in their turn. Most variations are harmful and are soon eliminated, but a few turn out to be beneficial and enhance survival and reproduction, and these will spread through the population. This process has allowed life to keep up with changing circumstances, generating a host of useful adaptations step by small step: devices to resist disease, eyes to see with, flowers to attract pollinators. Thanks to the

interplay of heredity, variation and natural selection life has pro-
liferated, become ever more diverse and colonized every habitable corner of the planet. Wherever you look, even in the depths
of the ocean and in hot dark rocks far beneath the surface, life
has made its home.

The theory of evolution makes rational sense of biology and
is supported by a great body of evidence; by contrast, not a
shred of objective evidence for divine creation has ever turned
up. Among scientists and laypersons who know something of
the natural world, agreement is all but unanimous. This is not
the case for the public at large. It is said that nearly half of all
Americans still hold that the earth and the life it bears were
created by divine command, just as we find them today, over a
span of six days less than ten thousand years ago. The situation
is better in Western Europe, but not by much. As to the Muslim
world and across the breadth of Asia and Africa, evolution (and
the scientific attitude in general) is confined to pockets here and
there. I well remember a long conversation with our guide on a
journey through Iran in 2000. He was an educated man, who
had studied in England, but the notion of evolution (particularly human evolution) was simply abhorrent to him; and so it
remains for the majority of his co-religionists.

Why has the nearly self-evident idea of evolution by natural
causes traveled so poorly? I believe that, at bottom, the reason
is that evolution denies that life has direction and purpose. We
humans are desperate to find meaning in our lives and in the
world around us. The theory of evolution, with its emphasis
on blind chance and selection for short-term advantage, asserts
that meaning and purpose are an illusion. As a scientist, I fully
subscribe to the modern version of evolution; all the evidence

supports it, none contradicts it. But as an occasional philosopher and increasingly concerned citizen, I fear that without the belief that our small lives have meaning in a greater scheme, we lose our moral moorings. And I wonder whether, absent a belief in a transcendent power that keeps the world on course, our kind of civilization can long endure.

The Tree of All Life

One of the chief accomplishments of evolutionary thinking has been to bring order to the profusion of living things. We make sense of disorder by grouping objects into categories (all buttons, for instance, or all blue flowers). In Darwin's time it was already common practice to assign organisms to bins nested within larger bins, based on similarities of form and function, as we still do today. Lions are placed in one species, tigers in another, but both are felines. Dogs are obviously quite different, but all three go into a larger bin that houses all mammals, and so on. Darwin gave the practical art of classification a larger purpose. He recognized that all organisms are related as members of a huge extended family, united by descent from a common ancestor; every species is a twig on a branch of a collective entity, the tree of all life. The object of our endeavors should therefore be to discover the natural classification, that which corresponds to the lines of descent. In time, it should be possible to draw up a tree on which every living thing occupies its proper place.

Partial trees that cover the animal and plant kingdoms could be constructed quite successfully using forms and functions as criteria of relatedness. It is much harder to envisage the tree as a whole, uniting organisms that apparently have nothing in common. How can one assess the relationship between trout and truffles, or petunias and pill bugs? Where do bacteria fit into the larger picture, and what should one make of the discovery that all cells fall into two great categories called prokaryotes and eukaryotes? This conundrum was not resolved until our own day, by introducing a new set of criteria to measure relationships: molecular sequences of large linear molecules, either the sequence of amino acids in proteins or the sequence of nucleotides in RNA and DNA. Like the organisms in which they are found, molecular sequences diverge and evolve over time. The order (sequence) of amino acids in the hemoglobin of lions and tigers are nearly identical, that of dogs is distinctly different, roundworm hemoglobin even more so. One can express the difference in numbers and state quantitatively how closely tigers and dogs are related. One can even use this distance to estimate how long ago these mammals diverged from their common ancestor. For example, it has been about six million years since the last common ancestor of humans and chimpanzees roamed the plains of East Africa.

Hemoglobin is a protein of animals, seldom found in plants; indeed, no single protein is found in all organisms. But all cellular beings contain ribosomes, the tiny machines that zip together amino acids to make proteins; and all ribosomes contain a particular species of RNA. By mapping nucleotide sequences of ribosomal RNA, the late Carl Woese (1928-2012) created the first universal tree of life in the 'eighties. The Big Tree is still a work in progress; it has been challenged, defended, revised, and augmented. Fig 10.1 shows one current version, which is likely to undergo further revision (relationships at the base of the tree are particularly uncertain). But the broad outlines are solid and have become the indispensable framework for inquiry into the nature and history of life.

Figure 10.1

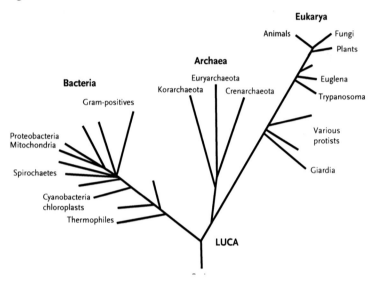

The universal tree of life, as inferred from the sequences of ribosomal RNA. The length of each branch measures evolutionary distance, not time. After Woese and others.

Reading the Tree as History

Biology will never be reduced to chemistry, for it is inherently a historical subject. Unlike chemistry, which deals with properties of matter that hold in all places and at all times, biology is about contingent events; they could have come out differently, and presumably are different on other inhabited planets. The tree of life is first of all a framework that displays the relationships between organisms – how one is related to another. But the universal tree is much more than that: It is a capsule summary of the history of life on earth. The vertical axis is a measure of "evolutionary distance", not of time, but those two are roughly proportional, and it is possible to attach approximate dates to key nodes. Take a closer look at Fig. 10.1, for what it proposes differs significantly from what biologists believed prior to the advent of molecular sequences, and even more so from what Darwin had in mind when he sketched the first tree in 1859.

Note first of all that the living world is divided into three great stems called domains: Bacteria, Archaea, and Eukarya (or Eucarya), all in capitals. The traditional biological kingdoms (animals, plants, fungi, and protists) survive as sub-divisions of the domains. Woese's first and most startling discovery (in the 1970s) was that the conventional term "prokaryotes" conflates two distinct classes of organisms that look much alike and have similar lifestyles, but are only distantly related. Domain Bacteria houses all the familiar bacteria that cycle nutrients, make cheese, and cause diseases such as cholera or tuberculosis. The Archaea were initially known only as bacteria that are found in peculiar and extreme environments, such as hot springs, brine ponds, and cows' rumens. But they turned out to be abundant in quite ordinary habitats such as soil and the open ocean, and they make up a substantial fraction of the biosphere. Both Bacteria and Archaea are unicellular microbes, too small to see without a good microscope. They are earth's most ancient inhabitants that first appeared as long ago as three billion years, and they are thought to stem directly from the last common ancestor of all life (dubbed LUCA), of whom we shall hear much more below. They flourished, diversified into the phyla we know today, and invented all basic cellular operations, including the ways of metabolism, heredity, and bioenergetics. Photosynthesis, for example, is a Bacterial invention, so Bacteria are ultimately responsible for the oxygen-rich atmosphere that supports all higher forms of life. Bacteria and Archaea still make up the bulk of the world's biomass, and the vast majority of its individual organisms; but it is striking that they have remained small and structurally prokaryotic, never giving rise to complex cells and multicellular organisms.

It's the Eukarya, and they alone, that explored the realm of larger size and advanced functions. That surely has to do with the eukaryotic ("true nucleus") mode of cell organization (Fig 10.2). Eukaryotic cells are much larger than prokaryotic ones, about one thousand-fold by volume, and display elaborate structural organization. A true nucleus with chromosomes and a bounding membrane, a ramifying network of intracellular membranes, and discrete organelles (mitochondria and chloroplasts) specialized for energy generation are all hallmarks of the eukaryotic order and are never seen in prokaryotes. The Eukarya cover a huge range of sizes, habitats and forms. The great majority are again unicellular microbes, such creatures as protozoa, algae, and yeast. But the domain also houses all the familiar animals (including ourselves), as well as plants and fungi. Any organism large enough to see with the naked eye is sure to be a eukaryote. Note that higher organisms make up only the terminal branches, little more than twigs on the universal tree of life. Most of the diversity of the eukaryotes and the bulk of their evolutionary history are microbial. Note furthermore that, while Eukarya make up a domain of their own, they are more closely related to the Archaea than to the Bacteria.

Figure 10.2

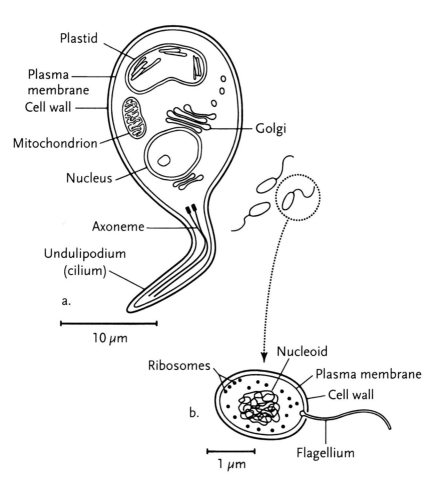

Eukaryotes and prokaryotes. Generalized sketches of of the structure of eukaryotic cells (a) and prokaryotic cells (b). Note the disparity of size and complexity. From Harold, 2014, with permission of The University of Chicago Press.

Figure 10.3

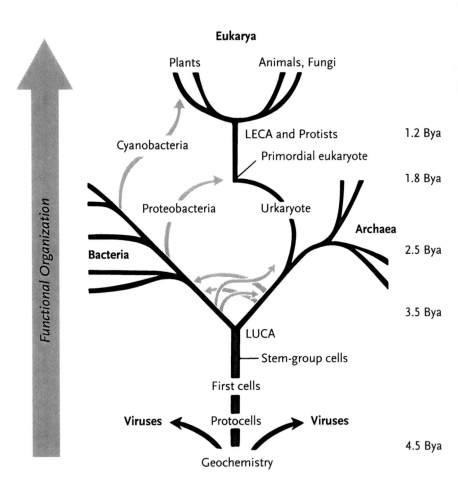

A brief history of life. The vertical axis denotes functional organization. Bya, billions of years ago. LUCA, last universal common ancestor; LECA, last common ancestor of extant eukaryotes. From Harold, 2014, with permission of The University of Chicago Press.

The rise of the eukaryotes marks a major shift in the evolution of life, from the exploration of biochemical space (the province of the prokaryotes) to that of functional organization. To emphasize this transition, Fig 10.3 shows a different version of the tree of life, one in which the vertical axis indicates the degree of structural organization (very roughly – there is no way to measure this). Here, it is the origin of eukaryotic cells that holds center stage. We do not know how that happened, which gives us plenty to argue about. Fig 10.3 presents one of the scenarios under debate, the one that presently seems to me the most plausible but is far from universally accepted. What we know for sure is that eukaryotic cells share many features (and genes) with both Bacteria and Archaea; and that both mitochondria and chloroplasts are descendants of Bacteria that were once free-living, but took up residence in the cytoplasm of the evolving eukaryotic cell ("endosymbiosis") and became the "power stations" that supply the eukaryotic cell with energy. Thus the eukaryotic cell is a "chimera", a consortium of cells of disparate origins.

The diagram (Fig. 10.3) proposes that the first such episode, the acquisition of Bacterial guests that gave rise to mitochondria, was a formative event in the genesis of the eukaryotic pattern of organization. It will have taken place nearly 2 billion years ago, a very long time indeed, but not nearly as distant as the diversification of Bacteria and Archaea. The nature of the cell that hosted the association is unknown and much disputed. I suspect that it was an early archaeon, one that possessed genes and proteins required for membrane remodeling and that made its living as a scavenger. Mitochondria opened access to new supplies of energy and initiated a line of evolution that led to the last common ancestor of all the existing eukaryotes (LECA), perhaps 1.7 billion years ago. The plant lineage stems from a separate episode of endosymbiosis, perhaps 1.2 billion years ago, when a species of photosynthetic Bacteria called cyanobacteria joined the first consortium. Cyanobacteria practice the kind of photosynthesis that generates oxygen as a by-product, and they were the precursors of all plant chloroplasts. Cyanobacteria are also the source of all the atmospheric oxygen on which the rest of us rely, and therefore, they can claim to have done more than anyone else to shape the planet as we know it. The protists, unicellular eukaryotes of which protozoa are the most familiar (e.g., *Paramecium* and amoebas), are the progeny of a radiation that took place about a billion years ago. Multicellular creatures such as worms and animals are more recent still; the most ancient of such forms appear about 0.7 billion years ago. The advent of humans is so recent that it does not register on the scale of this diagram.

Finally, note the peculiar status of viruses. Viruses are not cellular; they lack ribosomes (to reproduce, viruses commandeer the metabolic machinery of a host cell), and therefore, they have no place on a tree of life drawn primarily from the sequences of ribosomal RNA. But they are clearly part of the universe of living things, and not a peripheral part either. There is reason to believe that viruses are ancient, going back to the very dawn of life as shown in the diagram, but this is still an open question. The nature and status of viruses is perhaps the most glaring lacuna in our understanding of evolution.

How long is a billion years? Suppose you are an insomniac, counting sheep to put yourself to sleep; one second per sheep.

Well, it will take you nearly 32 years to rack up a billion, even without the occasional break – that's how long a billion is!

In Search of a Beginning

Perhaps the most penetrating insight into the nature of living things is that "life" is both plural and singular. Despite the overwhelming diversity of organisms past and present, all life is of one kind; it displays endless variations on a single molecular theme. Darwin intuited this 150 years ago, and molecular science established it as a fact. All organisms make their proteins from the same set of 20 amino acids, and their nucleic acids (RNA and DNA) from a ubiquitous set of 5 bases. A universal genetic code is employed by all to translate sequence information from the language of nucleic acids to that of proteins. Ribosomes, lipid bilayer membranes, ion-translocating ATPases, and ATP as energy currency are all part of the common endowment. In terms of the Darwinian paradigm, this means that all organisms share a common descent, and perhaps a single ancestor, who is known as LUCA (the last universal common, or cellular, ancestor).

With the formulation of the universal tree of life, the shadowy ancestor of us all acquired a habitation and became a proper subject for research. LUCA is represented on the tree by its first node, the bifurcation that divides Bacteria from Archaea. She is not the origin of life but stands for the first branch point on the tree and the most ancient event in life's history for which we have some evidence. For all the differences between them, Bacteria and Archaea are two variations on the universal themes. Some have argued that Archaea descend from Bacteria, or even the converse, but it is far more plausible that the two major stems share a common ancestry. LUCA is the nameplate on the door that opens unto what Woese once called "the murky realm of cell evolution".

What can one surmise about LUCA, an entity that no one has seen and that lived (by hypothesis) nearly four billion years ago? Not very much, and that with great trepidation, but speculation is ever so tempting. Judging by the fact that the basic molecular structures and operations of Bacteria and Archaea are variations on common themes, it seems safe to conclude that their precursors were already present in their common ancestor. (Note that there are also traits that occur in one stem but not in the other; photosynthesis is a Bacterial specialty, methane production an Archaeal one). So LUCA will have been an organism of sorts, endowed with genes, ribosomes, membranes, and some kind of energy conversion; simpler, perhaps, than contemporary cells but of the same general kind. But common ancestry does not necessarily imply a discrete common ancestor. One can make a good case that LUCA represents a stage before cells as we know them, when primordial molecular systems freely exchanged genes and evolved communally. Keep your saltshaker within reach! LUCA was presumably herself the product of a lengthy evolution, during which the basic machinery of cellular life fell into place. How that came about is essentially unknown and not accessible with current techniques. This makes the entire subject intensely frustrating, but also irresistibly challenging. The origin of cells, and of life, is the most consequential problem in all of biology. Until we figure out how life could have arisen by natural causes alone, we cannot rigorously exclude the claim that it required intervention by some higher power, and that is enough to give any rationalist conniptions.

The problem of life's origin has been especially attractive to chemists, often under the unspoken premise that once the critical molecules (RNA, proteins, lipids) are on hand, life will emerge spontaneously. The basic idea is that on the young earth all sorts of organic molecules would be formed under the influence of energy sources such as lightning and ultraviolet light. In the absence of living organisms to gobble them up, organic substances accumulated, generating a rich and savory "prebiotic soup". For at least 30 years, the favorite notion has been that a self-replicating molecule (most likely RNA) formed by chance in the soup. As it multiplied, it learned to clothe itself in accessory molecules that promoted replication or stability, and these were the nucleus around which the first living cells assembled themselves. There were always good reasons to be skeptical of this narrative, and its simpler versions have largely been abandoned. Alternative proposals seek the beginnings of life in metabolic cycles that arose spontaneously in the soup, or in lipid vesicles formed by abiotic reactions that trapped molecules such as nucleic acids. What all these notions have in common is that the molecules of life came first, and subsequently aggregated into primordial cells. The chemical approach lends itself to experiments that can be done in the lab. It has captured the imagination of scientists and the public, and generated an enormous literature, but never quite satisfied the skeptics.

A radical alternative, whose roots go clear back into the 19th century, seeks the origin of life in the inorganic world of geochemistry. Gases such as methane and hydrogen, exhaled by chemical reactions deep beneath the surface, could in principle reduce atmospheric carbon dioxide and support life. Microorganisms, strict anaerobes all, which make a living in this manner are well known, and some scientists maintain that their metabolic patterns have survived from the very dawn of cellular life. One possible venue for the beginning is submarine hydrothermal vents, specifically warm alkaline ones where fluids laden with hydrogen and methane well up and mix with the more acidulous waters of the ocean. Such vents construct towering spongy deposits, whose innumerable crannies and crevices could be sites where products of CO_2 reduction may accumulate and undergo further chemical transformations. These pores may even be the remote ancestors of cells and of the chemical reactions that underlie energy transduction. Like all other ideas about the origin of life, this one also has loose ends, a severe shortage of evidence, and a legion of critics. But it seems to me an idea worth keeping in mind.

In my opinion, any hypothesis that seeks to explain the origin of life by postulating an extensive menu of preformed organic molecules and essentially ignores the requirement for energy input is fundamentally off the mark. We should seek an alternative approach that, from the beginning, makes contact with life as it is: molecular systems organized into discrete pods that draw in matter and energy, grow and multiply, and evolve by variation and natural selection. I surmise that the long road to contemporary cells began with an energy source and rudimentary molecular networks driven by energy dissipation. A boundary that marked off the system from its surroundings must have been an early feature, and so must a source of chemical components to support expansion and multiplication. I envisage a purely chemical system, devoid of genes, functions, and structure, but subject to natural selection all the same. The quality under selection would have been stability, for that is essential for persistence; any system that cannot persist will soon vanish. The stability referred to here is not the solid, stolid stability of an unchanging rock, but the kinetic stability of a moving bicycle that stays upright so long as it keeps moving. The Israeli chemist Addy Pross, whose writings have done so much to clarify my own thinking, refers to the critical quality as "dynamic kinetic stability", and argues that this is the feature that opened a path to recognizable life.

In the beginning then, there was only chemistry, nothing to foretell "life". Chemistry began to morph into biology with the advent of the precursors to the characteristic molecules of life: proteins, lipids, and nucleic acids. Specialized molecules are both products of incipient life and causal to it, and would have initially served to enhance the system's kinetic stability. Simple abiotic molecules such as peptides and nucleotides took on their present-day functions in the storage and processing of information in tandem with the progressive refinement of cells. The driving force directed towards mounting functional organization would have been a rudimentary form of Darwin's triad of heredity, variation, and natural selection. Evolution and the mechanisms that underlie it are not part of the vocabulary of chemistry and physics, but are entirely consistent with the physical sciences. They point the way to a distinct realm of matter, which we designate as biology.

The foregoing sketch is not a hypothesis to explain the origin of life, merely a rough framework for thinking about the subject. To put flesh on those bones, one must offer answers to concrete questions. Chemical systems that are made up of multiple molecules and display dynamic kinetic stability are known, but appear to be very uncommon; and those that I have encountered have no obvious relevance to biology. What are the requirements for a plausible prebiotic system? Could it really undergo some form of evolution by natural selection? Are we searching for a rare, even singular event? And what would be a plausible energy source for such a system? There are not many; hydrothermal vents, anyone? Can one formulate a credible scenario for the genesis of life's universal molecules: DNA, RNA, proteins, membranes, also ribosomes, ion currents, and so on? We may never know the answer to these questions, which pertain to the particular course of our own evolutionary history. But one can hope to discover models to suggest how it could have happened. Like most scientists, I believe that life originated here on earth, by natural processes and without any need for intervention by transcendent powers. If such a path exists, it seems to be well hidden, very narrow, and perhaps blocked by obstacles that life overcame only by pure chance. I cannot think of any worthier purpose in life than to go and find it.

Does Evolution have a Purpose?

The universal tree of life unfolds a grand story, but hardly a simple one. The plot, as sketched in Fig. 10.3, turns on the rise of functional organization over time. How life began remains essentially unknown, but by about 3.2 billion years ago, it had reached a level of organization corresponding to prokaryotic cells. The fossils look just like today's Bacteria and Archaea, and they presumably made a living in much the same way. Prokaryotes or their antecedents invented all the essentials of life – the biochemical and genetic processes that make cellular life possible. They flourished, diversified prodigiously, and colonized every habitable nook and cranny; by most criteria, one must say that prokaryotes still rule the biosphere. But they remained small and structurally simple, and to all appearances, little changed over 3.2 billion years.

About 1.8 billion years ago, something dramatic happened: With the advent of eukaryotic cells, life took a great leap into a higher level of biological order, and that opened a new universe of possibilities to explore. It is surely of transcendent importance that all the complex, "higher" functions of life are seen only in eukaryotes: multicellular creatures with specialized organs, eggs and embryos, development, memory, speech, and mind. A few prokaryotes have experimented with multicellularity but never got very far. We do not know just what it is about eukaryotic cell organization that made all these advances possible, but the presence of energy-producing organelles (mitochondria and chloroplasts) surely played a large role. Within the eukaryotic stem, there has been a dramatic increase in functional organization over time: first protists and green algae, later multicellular plants, fungi, and animals. The climb presently culminates in ourselves, *Homo sapiens*, whose mental powers vastly exceed those of all other creatures. Yes, I know, our species is not living up to its name, may even close out the entire biotic adventure, and so any scale that puts humans on top gives many of my colleagues the shudders. But there is no escaping the obvious. The upward trend in organization, particularly in the eukaryotic lineage, is neither uniform nor universal but so plain overall that it makes no sense to deny it.

How can one account for an upward trend in functional organization, however fitful and episodic, in the face of the universal tendency (mandated by thermodynamics) of things to fall apart over time? Among biologists there is little doubt that this can happen only in the context of cells and organisms, not of free molecules, and that the driving force is Darwin's ramp of heredity, variation, and natural selection. There is nothing in the theory of evolution itself that prescribes a global trend towards greater complexity and higher organization; it predicts only that organisms that do well in their time and place will persist, reproduce, and leave offspring that will be successful in their turn. But many of the heritable variations that natural selection has favored because they improve performance do, in fact, entail more complex organization (think eyes or legs). The reason is the same as that which makes my Subaru so much more elaborate than a Model T: It works better. Let me be careful not to oversimplify. Not all features of organisms should be regarded as adaptations, and their complexity is not always due to natural selection. The dramatic rise of the Eukarya, apparently beginning with some kind of fusion or merger of different cell types, stands way outside traditional ideas about evolution by small incremental steps. But the fundamental principle of heredity, variation, and natural selection continues to apply, and we know of no other rational way to explain the build-up of functional organization over time.

Do the same well-honed principles also explain the origin of cellular organization in the first place? Here we stand on far less secure ground. Heredity, variation, and natural selection only operate efficiently in systems that are highly organized to begin with. Basic cell operations such as genes, ribosomes, transcription, translation, and membranes studded with transport carriers and reliant on ion currents, all require integrated cells of some sort. One can only make genes with the help of proteins, but genes are required to specify the structure of proteins. Both are needed to make working membranes, yet without enclosure, the evolution of genes and proteins is unimaginable. It is simply not clear how to account for the origin of these sophisticated operations, and that is why the origin of cells remains a mystery rather than puzzle. We can be confident that evolutionary mechanisms had a hand in shaping cells, no less than plants and animals, for we see their traces in the sequences of all macromolecules. But that does not quite answer the question, nor set to rest all doubts. The fact is that the origin of cellular organization remains lost in the murk that covers all beginnings, and it is presently only accessible to speculation and reflection.

The belief that the magnificent history of life is wholly the result of chance variation winnowed by selection for short-term advantage has become almost an article of faith among biologists, but makes many others uncomfortable, and me also. Is this really all there is to "The Greatest Show on Earth" – no direction, no purpose, no goal, and no meaning? Must we ultimately subscribe to the bleak assessment of the physicist Steven Weinberg, that "the more [evolution] is comprehensible, the more it also seems pointless"? I share the dislike for this conclusion, but the facts cannot simply be wished away. There is no evidence whatever for direction, goal, or the guiding hand of a higher power. Moreover, given all that we have discovered, there is no obvious way in which any directive force could be brought to bear.

It is only when we view the history of life on our little planet in the context of the universe at large that hints of a wider meaning begin to emerge. The history of the universe as we currently understand it tells of the continuous unfolding of structure, order, and complexity; it is erratic, variable, local rather than global, but relentless. The narrative begins with the Big Bang and winds its way through the formation of atomic nuclei and chemical elements to simple molecules. It speaks of the formation of stars, planets, and moons, of galaxies and structures on a yet larger scale, and of continuing expansion. There seems to be a tendency towards order that is built into the very fabric of things, and the story of life on earth is but a single chapter in that ongoing tale. Are we humans alone in the vastness of the universe, speckled with billions of stars and solar systems? It seems unlikely – rare, probably, but not unique. Cosmology is far removed from the concerns of most biological scientists, let alone the general public. But it may turn out that only through that prism can we view the story of life as a whole – as it is, not as we wish it were. And with that we must be content.

Epilogue: Desiderata

Whether or not we realize it, the modern world is steeped in science and the fruits of science. The technology that increasingly rules our lives is not like the crafts of olden days; more and more, it is based on the discoveries and the mind-set of science. One cannot imagine air conditioning, scotch tape, non-stick cookware, hip replacements, birth-control pills, herbicides, airplanes, missiles, and robots without a real understanding of how the world works. Science and technology are not the same thing, but ever since the industrial revolution, the conceptual and the practical have become intertwined, one stimulating the other. Progress in both has been astonishing and often alarming, and they are transforming the world at an ever-faster clip.

It never ceases to surprise me how few people understand the symbiotic relationship between science and the way we live now. As an academic, basic scientist, I have often been asked to explain what my kind of science is good for and have found it all but impossible to break through the wall of incomprehension. People can relate to cancer research, but "bioenergetics"? Yet bioenergetics is an essential part of how cells work, and therefore, it indirectly informs what oncologists do. As early as the 17th century, Francis Bacon understood that "experiments of light are to be as highly prized as experiments of fruit", so let me try once more.

One of the stars in the economic firmament is the biotechnology industry, which employs hundreds of thousands worldwide and offers a large range of products that simply did not exist half a century ago. The list includes human growth hormone and insulin, a shelf of medications and vaccines, diagnostic kits for dozens of maladies, biofuel from cultivated algae, even a nutritious food called Quorn made from fungi (popular in the U.K. but little known on this side of the pond). There will be much more to come. Where did this industry come from? The conscious search for useful or marketable products played a part, but what made it all possible is the growing knowledge of how living things work, microbes in particular. And none of that would have come about without some humble beginnings – petri plates and agar and pure strains of bacteria, which underpin our command of biochemistry and genetics. We stand on the shoulders of six generations of researchers. Some labored with practical goals in mind (Pasteur took chances to help patients at risk of from rabies, not to found immunology), but much of the work was undertaken solely for the sake of understanding, without any intention of someday engineering *E.coli* to produce insulin. Only in about 1970, did it dawn on some scientists (specifically Herbert Boyer and Stanley Cohen) that the tools were at hand to transfer genes from one bacterium to another. They went on to found the first biotech firm and laid the foundations for a whole industry. One can tell similar tales with less benign outcomes, such as the origins of the atomic bomb or the tide of plastic trash that now fouls the high seas, but the point is the same. Today's technology, medicine, agriculture, and warfare are all grounded in science and would never have come to be as we find them but for the scientific revolution that began 300 years ago.

By and large, folks in the West (and America in particular) embrace the burgeoning technology, and even those who know little of science take much science for granted and welcome it into their lives. Ghosts, witches, and the Devil are topics for entertainment, not for dread. We know that the earth is round, spins on its axis, and travels around the sun. We expect sickness, storms, and earthquakes to have natural and comprehensible causes and need not credit the will of some inscrutable deity. And most of us, though not all, accept that reason and evidence outweigh authority and tradition. No one would describe the American public as scientifically literate, but neither do we still live in the Middle Ages.

Many of the questions we confront in our private and public lives have a scientific dimension, and it is sometimes asserted that therefore people must have enough understanding of science to make informed decisions. That strikes me as unrealistic. How can anyone, scientists themselves included, have the technical knowledge to judge the benefits and risks of genetically modified foods, and also what we should do about climate change, not to mention whether vaccinations increase the risk of autism?

All of us, scientists and laypersons alike, must rely on the judgment of others, and the challenge is to choose a trustworthy source of information and advice. That is not easy, but not altogether impossible; look for the factual basis of claims and assertions, a judicial attitude, and be skeptical of anyone with simple answers and an axe to grind. Above all, remember that you may be mistaken!

Here is where some real acquaintance with science comes in handy, for of all human endeavors, science alone strives for objective knowledge. It is not the facts of science, not even its insights, but its rational, critical spirit that helps one navigate the morass of information, misinformation, and downright falsehood that clutters up our lives and overwhelms the judgment. Individually, scientists like everyone else are fallible, gullible, and corruptible. Even the practice as a whole is far from error-proof: after all, on the historical time scale, almost all scientific theories were eventually discarded. All the same, only science has over time shown itself able to make successful predictions upon which we can build a firm understanding of how the world works. I see little point in calling for a larger role for science in the school curriculum. To be sure, science is important, but so are history and geography and basic life skills, and there is only so much time and energy to go 'round. But I would wish for more emphasis on the outlook that sets apart science at its best: never-ending curiosity, the insistence that all knowledge is tentative, respect for evidence, and the rejection of all claims to Truth writ large. Few people are born with that attitude, it has to be learned over time, but one improves with practice. Science is more than a way to know the world: It is THE way that has made the world we live in today, and barring some global catastrophe, it will be the way of our future.

Notes

Chapter 1:

There is an enormous amount of literature about the state of Israel and its place in the world. One book that I particularly admire *is My Promised Land — The Triumph and Tragedy of Israel* by Ari Shavit (2014).

Chapter 4:

The following publications track the evolution of my scientific interests:

Articles

1. F.M. Harold, 1966. Inorganic polyphosphates in biology: Structure, metabolism and function. *Bacteriological Reviews*, 30: 772 - 794.

2. F.M. Harold, 1972. Conservation and transformation of energy by bacterial membranes. *Bacteriological Reviews*, 36: 172 - 230.

3. F.M. Harold, 1977. Ion currents and physiological functions in microorganisms. *Annual Review of Microbiology*, 31: 181 - 203.

4. F.M. Harold, 1990. To shape a cell: An inquiry into the causes of morphogenesis of microorganisms. *Microbiological Reviews*, 54: 381 - 431.

5. F.M. Harold, 1995. From morphogenes to morphogenesis. *Microbiology* (Reading, UK), 141: 2765 - 2778.

6. F.M. Harold and P.C. Maloney, 1996. Energy transduction by ion currents. In: Escherichia coli and Salmonella typhimurium. F.C. Neidhardt et al., eds, second edition, *American Society for Microbiology*, Vol 1, 283 - 306.

7. F.M. Harold, 1997. How hyphae grow: Morphogenesis explained? *Protoplasma*, 197: 237 - 247.

8. F.M. Harold, 2001. Postscript to Schroedinger: So what is life? *ASM News*, 67: 611 - 616.

9. F.M. Harold, 2002. Force and compliance: Rethinking morphogenesis in walled cells. *Fungal Genetics and Biology*, 37: 271 - 282.

10. F.M. Harold, 2005: Molecules into cells: Specifying spatial architecture. *Microbiology and Molecular Biology Reviews*, 69: 544 – 564.

Books

1. F.M. Harold, 1986. *The Vital Force – A Study of Bioenergetics.* W.H. Freeman, 577 pages.

2. F.M. Harold, 2001. *The Way of the Cell: Molecules, Organisms and the Order of Life.* Oxford University Press, 305 pages.

3. F.M. Harold, 2014. *In Search of Cell History: The Evolution of Life's Building Blocks.* University of Chicago Press, 303 pages.

Chapter 5:
John Prebble and Bruce Weber have written an excellent biography of Peter Mitchell, which can also serve as a history of the chemiosmotic revolution: *Wandering in the Gardens of the Mind: Peter Mitchell and the Making of Glynn;* Oxford University Press, 2003.

Key articles on the chemiosmotic revolution include the following:
1. P. Mitchell, 1966. Chemiosmotic coupling in oxidative and photosynthetic phosphorylation. *Biological Reviews of the Cambridge Philosophical Society,* 41: 445 - 502.

2. P. Mitchell, 1976. Vectorial chemistry and the molecular mechanisms of chemiosmotic coupling. *Biochemical Society Transactions,* 4: 399 - 430.

3. P. Mitchell, 1979. David Keilin's respiratory chain concept and its chemiosmotic consequences. *Science,* 206: 1148 - 1159.

Chapter 7:

What is science that it should so possess some people, alienate others and transform the way we perceive the world? Among the general books that I have enjoyed are the following: Jacob Bronowski, *The Common Sense of Science* (1951) and Peter Medawar, *Pluto's Republic* (1982).

For further reading see: Thomas Kuhn, *The Structure of Scientific Revolutions* (second edition, 1970); Karl Popper, *Objective Knowledge — An Evolutionary Approach* (1972); and David Wootton, *The Invention of Science — A New History of the Scientific Revolution* (2015).

My understanding of the Middle East, and of the world in general, has been much influenced by the writings of Bernard Lewis, specifically, *The Middle East – A Brief History of the Last 2000 Years* (1995), and *What Went Wrong: The Clash between Islam and Modernity in the Middle East* (2002); also by Samuel P. Huntington, *The Clash of Civilizations and the Remaking of World Order* (1996).

Chapter 8:

What is Life? Philosophers and scholars have grappled with this question for centuries, and now scientists are weighing in. The modern classic, which inspired many young scientists of the post-war era including myself, is *What is Life ?*, by Erwin Schroedinger (1944). More recent and reasonably accessible treatments include: W.S. Beck, *Modern Science and the Nature of Life* (1957); Jacques Monod, *Chance and Necessity* (1971); Francois Jacob, *The Logic of Life: A History of Heredity* (1973);

Renato Dulbecco, *The Design of Life* (1975); Lynn Margulis and Dorion Sagan, *What is Life?*; John Maynard Smith, *The Problems of Life* (1986); and of course, Franklin M. Harold, *The Way of the Cell – Molecules, Organisms and the Order of Life* (2001).

Monod and Beck are quoted from the books listed above. Rupert Riedl's groundbreaking work is *Order in Living Organisms* (1978). For Stuart Kauffman, see: *The Origins of Order: Self Organization and Selection in Evolution* (1993) and *Investigations* (2000).

Chapter 9:
Sources for bioenergetics and chemiosmotics are listed in Notes for Chapters 4 and 5; Jacob and Dulbecco in those for Chapter 8.

It is surprisingly difficult to find a contemporary statement of the gene-centered view of life; it's just what everyone knows! The most articulate exponents are still: Richard Dawkins (*The Selfish Gene*, 2nd edition, 1976; *River Out of Eden*, 1995; *Climbing Mount Improbable*, 1996) and Daniel Dennett (*Darwin's Dangerous Idea*, 1993). Neither of them tries to tackle findings that cast doubt on the received dogma. A full-throated endorsement does come from J. Craig Venter, *Life at the Speed of Light – From the Double Helix to the Dawn of Digital Life* (2013).

The technical articles from Venter's group are the following:
C. Lartigue et al., *Science*, 317: 633 - 638, 2007;

D. G. Gibson et al., *Science*, 329: 52 - 56, 2010; and

C.A. Hutchinson et al., *Science*, 351: 1414, 2016.

The holistic or "systems" view of life has been presented several times. In addition to my own writings (Harold, 2001 and 2014), see: Dennis Noble, *The Music of Life – Biology Beyond the Genome* (2006) and Fritjof Capra and Pier Luigi Luisi, *The Systems View of Life – A Unifying Vision* (2014).

Chapter 10:
The case for evolution has been made ever since Darwin, recently in the context of the rancorous dispute over "intelligent design". See, for example, J.A. Coyne, *Why Evolution is True* (2009) and Richard Dawkins, *The Greatest Show on Earth – The Evidence for Evolution* (2009).

Cell evolution is an intensely active field that features many technical papers but not much in the way of books. The only systematic treatment that I am aware of is my own, *In Search of Cell History – The Evolution of Life's Building Blocks* (2014). See also Jan Sapp, *The New Foundations of Evolution* (2009); Eugene V. Koonin, *The Logic of Chance – The Nature and Origin of Biological Evolution* (2012); and especially, Nick Lane, *The Vital Question – Energy, Evolution and the Origins of Complex Life* (2015). For the geological dimension, do not miss Andrew Knoll, *Life on a Young Planet* (2003).

The traditional premise that evolution is in some fundamental sense progressive has become highly controversial. See, for example, S.J. Gould, *Full House – The Spread of Excellence from Plato to Darwin* (1996). By contrast, Nick Lane takes it for granted in *Life Ascending – The Ten Great Inventions of Evolution* (2009).

There is a shelf-full of books on the origin of life. In addition to Koonin and Lane, above, I have been impressed by Robert Hazen, *Gen.e.sis* (2005), and especially by Addy Pross, *What is Life – How Chemistry becomes Biology* (2012, and later technical writings).

Glossary

Adaptation: In evolution, any change in the structure or functioning of an organism that makes it better suited to its environment.

Adenosine diphosphate (ADP): See adenosine triphosphate.

Adenosine triphosphate (ATP): The universal energy currency of living organisms. The molecule consists of adenine, ribose, and three phosphoryl groups; successive release of phosphate gives rise to adenosine diphosphate (ADP) and adenosine monophosphate (AMP).

ADP: See adenosine triphosphate.

Amino acids: Small, water-soluble organic compounds that possess both a carboxyl group (-COOH) and an amino group (-NH$_2$). Proteins are polymers made up of a characteristic set of twenty amino acids.

Archaea: Microbial clade originally defined by ribosomal RNA sequences and associated with extreme environments, now known to be widespread. Archaea constitute one of the three domains of life.

Archaeon: An organism classified in the domain Archaea.

ATP: See adenosine triphosphate.

ATP synthase: A class of complex enzymes pivotal to biological energy transduction, which link ATP chemistry in the cytoplasm to the translocation of protons (sometimes Na^+) across membranes. In bacteria, mitochondria, and chloroplasts, ATP synthases catalyze ATP synthesis during oxidative and photosynthetic phosphorylation.

Bacteria: Diverse microbial domain that includes most of the familiar lineages, as well as the ancestors of both mitochondria and plastids. When spelled with a lower case b, refers to the traditional informal term for prokaryotes.

Catalyst: A substance that increases the rate of a chemical reaction without itself undergoing permanent chemical change. Enzymes are the chief catalysts in biochemical reactions.

Cell: The structural and functional unit of living organisms. Cell size varies, but most are microscopic (0.001 to 0.1 mm). Many organisms consist of but a single cell (bacteria and most protists); others are multicellular (fungi, plants, and animals).

Cell wall: The strong and relatively rigid envelope of many cells, external to the plasma membrane. Cells of plants, fungi, many protists, and most bacteria are walled; animal cells are not.

Chemiosmotic theory: The proposal that biological energy transactions are effected by ion currents.

Chloroplast: A membrane-bound organelle in cells of plants and green algae that contains chlorophyll and is the locus of photosynthesis.

Chromosome: A thread-like structure found in cell nuclei, which carries genes in linear array.

Complexity: The condition of a system made up of multiple interacting parts, whose behavior is not easily deduced from the properties of those components.

Cyanobacteria: A phylum of Bacteria that is characterized by photosynthesis of the same kind as that of plastids.

Cytoplasm: The jelly-like material that fills cellular space, exclusive of the nucleus and other organelles.

Cytoskeleton: A network of microscopic filaments and tubules that pervades the cytoplasm of both eukaryotic and prokaryotic cells. Its functions include motility, cell division, and secretion.

Deoxyribonucleic acid: See DNA.

DNA (Deoxyribonucleic acid): A nucleic acid composed of two intertwined polynucleotide chains; the sugar is deoxyribose. DNA is the genetic material of all cells and of many viruses.

Domain : The highest level of biological classification. The three domains are Archaea, Bacteria, and Eukarya.

E. coli (Escherichia coli): A normal inhabitant of the human gut, classified in the phylum *Proteobacteria.* Of all living organisms, it is the one most fully understood.

Emergence: The appearance of new properties in a system that were not present nor easily predictable from the properties of the components.

Endosymbiosis: A symbiosis in which one of the partners (the endosymbiont) resides within the cytoplasm of the other.

Energy: The capacity to do work. In biology, it is the capacity to drive processes that do not occur spontaneously, such as the synthesis of complex molecules.

Enzyme: A protein that acts as a catalyst in biochemical reactions.

Eukarya (Eucarya): The domain of life that contains all eukaryotes, whether unicellular or multicellular.

Eukaryotes (Eucaryotes): Organisms whose genetic material is enclosed in a true, membrane-bound nucleus. Eukaryotic cells also typically have a cytoskeleton, internal membranes, and organelles.

Evolution: The doctrine that living organisms arose from unlike ancestors by small changes over long periods of time.

Fermentation: A biochemical pathway that breaks down organic substances, in the absence of oxygen, with production of metabolites and usable energy.

Flagellum: A relatively long, whip-like structure present on the surface of many cells and serving as an organ of motility.

Gene: A unit of heredity, usually consisting of a stretch of DNA that codes for some biological function.

Genome: The total gene complement of an organism; more precisely, all the genes carried on a single set of chromosomes.

Glycolysis: The sequence of reactions by which sugar is converted to ethanol in the absence of oxygen.

Holism: The doctrine that a biological system is more than the sum of its components. To understand the whole, one must know its parts, but that dissection always leaves an unexplained residue that turns on relationships among those parts.

Ion: An atom or molecule bearing an electric charge. One example is the hydrogen ion, or proton.

Ion current: A flux of ions across a membrane.

Kingdom: In taxonomy, a high level of classification. Traditional kingdoms include animals, fungi, and plants.

Last universal common ancestor: A hypothetical organism ancestral to all three domains of life. Commonly abbreviated LUCA.

Lateral Gene Transfer: Transfer of genes by mechanisms other than cell reproduction.

LECA: Last eukaryotic common ancestor; the last common ancestor of all existing eukaryotes.

Lipid: Any of a diverse group of organic compounds found in living organisms that are insoluble in water but soluble in organic solvents such as chloroform or benzene. Examples include fats, oils, steroids, and terpenes.

LUCA: See last universal common ancestor.

Machine: An ensemble of interconnected parts that harnesses energy to the performance of work.

Membranes: In this book, the thin sheets made up of lipids and proteins that form the boundaries of cells, organelles, and intracellular compartments.

Metabolism: The sum of the chemical reactions that take place in a living organism. Compounds that take part in, or are formed by, these reactions are called *metabolites*. A sequence of reactions that generates (or degrades) a metabolite is considered a *metabolic pathway*.

Mitochondrion: An organelle of eukaryotic cells that is the locus of respiration and oxidative phosphorylation.

Mitosis: The division of a cell to form two daughter cells, each of which has a nucleus containing the same number and kind of chromosomes as the mother cell.

Molecule: The smallest unit of any compound, consisting of atoms (several or many) held together by chemical bonds. For example, a molecule of water (H_2O) consists of two hydrogen atoms and one of oxygen.

Morphogenesis: The development of form and structure in an organism.

Mutant: An organism or a gene that has undergone a mutation.

Mutation: A heritable change in the genetic material of a cell that may cause it and its descendants to differ from the normal in appearance or behavior.

Nuclear membrane: The membrane that delimits the nucleus and regulates the flow of materials between nucleus and cytoplasm. By definition, eukaryotic nuclei are bounded by a membrane; prokaryotic ones are not.

Nucleic acid: A large and complex biological molecule consisting of a chain of nucleotides. There are two types: deoxyribonucleic acid (DNA) and ribonucleic acid (RNA).

Nucleotides: The basic building blocks of nucleic acids. Each nucleotide consists of a nitrogenous base, a sugar, and one or more phosphate groups.

Nucleus/Nucleoid: The large, membrane-bound body embedded in the cytoplasm of eukaryotic cells that contains the genetic material. A nucleoid is the corresponding structure in prokaryotic cells, which is not enclosed in a membrane.

Order: A state in which the components are arranged in a regular, comprehensible, or predictable manner. Various degrees of order are represented by the letters of the alphabet, the arrangement of a keyboard, and the sequence of amino acids in a protein.

Organelle: A minute structure within a cell that has a particular function. Examples include the nucleus, mitochondria, and flagella.

Organism: An individual living creature, either unicellular or multicellular.

Organization: Purposeful or functional order, as in the arrangement of the parts of a bicycle or a skeleton.

Oxidative phosphorylation: The chief mechanism of ATP production in aerobic organisms. The enzymatic generation of ATP coupled to the transfer of electrons from a substrate to oxygen.

Peptide: One of a large class of organic compounds consisting of two or more amino acids linked by peptide bonds.

Phagocytosis: The process by which cells engulf and digest minute food particles.

Phospholipid: One of a group of lipids that contains both a phosphate group and one or more fatty acids.

Photosynthesis: The chemical process by which green plants (and many other organisms) use the energy of light to synthesize organic compounds from CO_2 and water.

Phylogeny: An evolutionary relationship among organisms or their parts (e.g. genes).

Phylum: A category used in the classification of animals, such as the phyla *Protozoa* or *Mollusca*. In the classification of plants, the term "division" is preferred. Both terms are used to designate the major categories of Bacteria and Archaea.

Plasma membrane (cytoplasmic membrane): The membrane that forms the outer limit of a cell and regulates the flow of material into and out of the cell.

Plastid: General term for the organelles that carry out photosynthesis in eukaryotic cells.

Polymer: A molecule or complex composed of repeating elements (monomers). For example, proteins are polymers of amino acids.

Polynucleotide: Any polymer of nucleotides, including DNA and RNA.

Polypeptide: A peptide containing more than ten amino acids, commonly a hundred or more. All proteins are polypeptides.

Prokaryotes (Procaryotes): Organisms whose genetic material is not separated from the cytoplasm by a nuclear membrane. More generally, it denotes a grade of cellular organization lacking a true nucleus and most organelles. Both Bacteria and Archaea belong to this grade.

Protein: A large molecule consisting of one or more polypeptide chains; the molecular mass ranges from 6,000 daltons to the millions.

Protist: A member of the kingdom Protista, which includes the unicellular eukaryotic organisms and some multicellular lineages derived from them.

Protocell: In this book, a hypothetical pre-cellular entity that lacks genes and encoded gene products such as proteins.

Protoplasm: See Cytoplasm.

Protozoa: In this book, used generically to designate non-photo-synthetic protists, such as amoebas or ciliates.

Redox chain: A cascade of enzymes that carry out successive steps of reduction and oxidation. The respiratory chain is an example.

Reductionism: The doctrine that the properties of a complex system can be largely (or even wholly) understood in terms of its simpler parts or components.

Replication: The production of an exact copy. Usually employed in reference to the replication of DNA, in which one strand provides a template for the formation of a complementary strand, which is then copied once more to reproduce the original.

Respiration: The utilization of oxygen. In cell biology, it refers to the oxidative degradation of organic substances with the production of metabolites and energy. Oxygen usually serves as the oxidant, but sulfate or nitrate sometimes take its place in "anaerobic respiration".

Respiratory chain: The biochemical basis of respiration; a cascade of proteins and other metabolites that carries electrons from substrates to oxygen in aerobic cells.

Ribonucleic acid: See RNA.

Ribosomes: Intracellular organelles that carry out protein synthesis, found in all cells. They are composed of several species of RNA and some fifty proteins.

RNA (Ribonucleic acid): A nucleic acid made up of polynucleotide chains whose sugar is ribose. Examples include ribosomal RNA, transfer RNA, and messenger RNA.

Self-assembly: A mode of self-organization in which supramolecular order emerges from the association of molecules without input of either external information or energy. Examples include the polymerization of tubulin into microtubules.

Self-organization: In this book, the emergence of supramolecular order from the interaction of many molecules that obey only local rules, without reference to an external template or global plan.

Sequence: The order of amino acids in a protein or of nucleotides in a nucleic acid. The determination of that order is referred to as *sequencing.*

Species: In taxonomy, a group of similar and closely related individuals that can usually breed among themselves.

Symbiosis: Living together; an interaction between individuals of different species that is beneficial to both partners.

System: An entity composed of elements that interact or are related to one another in some definite manner. A bicycle and a cell are systems; a lump of granite is not.

Taxonomy: The practice or science of classification.

Transcription: Assembly of an RNA molecule complementary to a stretch of DNA. This is the first step in protein synthesis and represents the transfer of sequence information from DNA to RNA.

Transduction: Conversion, as in the transduction of one kind of energy into another.

Translation: Assembly of a protein by a ribosome, using messenger RNA to specify the order of the amino acids.

Transport system: One or more proteins whose function is to carry substances across a membrane. Also known as carriers.

Vectorial: Having a direction in space.

Vesicle: A small, membrane-bound sac (usually filled with fluid) within the cytoplasm of a living cell.

Virus: A particle too small to be seen with the light microscope or to be trapped by filters, but capable of reproduction within a living cell. Viruses have very limited metabolic capacities and are obligatory intracellular parasites.

Work: A process that runs counter to the spontaneous direction of events. For example, protein synthesis represents work but their degradation does not.

CPSIA information can be obtained
at www.ICGtesting.com
Printed in the USA
LVOW09*0013180317
527209LV00010BA/146/P